One year at Book Number thrëe

By

Victoria Blashford Snell

Celia Brooks Brown

Ursula Ferrigno

Jennifer Joyce

Decorated by Selina Snow

PRYOR PUBLICATIONS
WHITSTABLE, WALSALL
AND WINCHESTER

75 Dargate Road, Yorkletts, Whitstable,
Kent CT5 3AE, England.
Tel. & Fax: (01227) 274655
E-mail: alan@pryor-publish.clara.net
http://home.clara.net/pryor-publish
Kent Exporter of the Year Awards Winner 1998

Specialists in Facsimile Reproductions
MEMBER OF
INDEPENDENT PUBLISHERS GUILD

Front cover illustration by Barbara Dorf
Compiled by Rosie Kindersley
Published by Pryor Publications
for
Books for Cooks© 1997
4 Blenheim Crescent, W11 1NN.
Tel: (0171) 221 1992/8102   Fax: (0171) 221 1517
E-mail: info@booksforcooks.com

BOOKS
FOR
COOKS
1994

Reprinted 1998–1999

One Year At Books For Cooks Nos. 1 & 2
are available from Books For Cooks
at £5 each including postage

Typeset in Garamond by Paul Hanks
Tel. & Fax: (01227) 262735

ISBN 0 946014 62 0

A CIP Record for this book is available from the British Library

Printed and bound by
Whitstable Litho

Whitstable
Kent

CONTENTS

INTRODUCTION

It all began in 1995, one winter Sunday afternoon, when a small crowd of cookery enthusiasts gathered together in this the smallest restaurant in London, the test kitchen at Books for Cooks. They had come to see our rising star Ursula demonstrate the best of Italian vegetarian cooking. We'd noticed the increasing number of enquiries about cookery courses and so stuck up a notice in the shop advertising a few. People came and, much to our astonishment, they kept coming. Yes, I say astonishment, because things didn't always run according to plan in those early days. Squashed together like veritable sardines, crammed in between the bookshelves and practically in the kitchen with the pots and pans, they emerged from the workshop almost cooked themselves with the combined heat of the oven and the stove, often damp with the drips of condensed steam which dropped from the glass roof on account of the boiling pans, probably reeling with the multitude of food scents and savours, and surely exhausted with the barrage of information and activity we launched at them. Sometimes the classes lasted in the region of two hours, sometimes up to four, like the time when the chef and first time demonstrator (me, I'm afraid) was so ambitious with the mountain of fish he bought that some of it had to be taken back and finished at home by the students. But there was magic in the air and word of the workshops began to spread.

From these certainly humble beginnings, I think you'll agree we've come a long way. With Heidi as the driving force, we took the workshops from downstairs to upstairs at Book for Cooks, with a brand new demonstration kitchen. The classes divide into three progams. **THE BASICS** are my province; they take place once a week and guide students through the fundamental techniques of various areas of cookery — sauces, chopping, pastry, bread, sausage-making or outdoor cooking, to name but a few. For **THE ENTERTAINING SERIES** specialist demonstrators and authors tackle a particular theme such as Moroccan, Thai, Party Food or Christmas with contemporary and classic recipes, and essential tips and know-how. Lastly, there is THE ITALIAN KITCHEN which focuses on the culinary specialities of Italy (*la pasta, le verdure, i gnocchi, i dolci, le pane, gli antipasti,* for example) and taught by our own *enfant terrible* Ursula with such special knowledge and real passion.

Now back to the test kitchen. I'd like to introduce you to Celia, who joins our three faithful regular cooks in authoring this year's book. She walked in the shop one day and enchanted us with her bright enthusiasm. Although she started off working in the bookshop, she soon graduated to the test kitchen where her eclectic and inspired style of almost vegetarian cookery is always the highlight of the week. I'm sure you can perfectly see why I sometimes feel I'm in the middle of a culinary Charlie's Angels, a lone chef surrounded by all this dazzling feminine talent!

Well, another year has gone by at Books for Cooks like a flash in the pan. And it still smells good. A year of testing and tasting has reaped a rich harvest from the culinary crop of recipes and I hope you'll agree that this, our third book, is another great vintage.

Soyez sage.

Treville Eric

Our Favourite Cookbooks of the Year

Blakes, Andrew Blake. Victoria: William Heinemann Australia
The Book of Jewish Food, Claudia Roden. New York: Alfred A. Knopf
Chez Panisse Vegetables, Alice Waters. New York: HarperCollins
The Cook's Companion, Stephanie Alexander. Victoria: Viking
The Dean & Deluca Cookbook, David Rosengarten. New York: Random House
A Flavour of Tuscany, Vivienne Gonley. London: Headline
Four Star Desserts, Emily Luchetti. New York: HarperCollins
From Anna's Kitchen, Anna Thomas. London: Penguin Books
Healthy Mediterranean Cooking, Rena Salaman. London: Frances Lincoln
More Taste Than Time, Annie Bell. London: Ebury Press
Patricia Wells at Home in Provence, Patricia Wells. New York: Scribner
Real Fast Vegetarian, Ursula Ferrigno. London: Metro Books
Savoring Spices and Herbs, Julie Sahni. New York: William Morrow
The Tate Cookbook, Michael Driver & Jenny Linford. London: Tate Gallery Publishing
Two Fat Ladies, Jennifer Paterson & Clarissa Dickson Wright. London: Ebury Press

Soups

CREAM OF FENNEL SOUP

The light creaminess and subtle anise flavours of this recipe from *The Tate Cookbook* by Michael Driver & Jenny Linford make for absolute soup perfection.

2 large fennel bulbs, chopped
1 leek, chopped
1 onion, peeled and chopped
1oz/2 tbsp/30g butter
salt and pepper
1½ pints/3¾ cups/900ml boiling chicken or
vegetable stock
4 tbsp double/heavy cream
dill sprigs to garnish

Melt the butter and gently stew the vegetables with a large pinch of salt and the lid on over a low heat until softened, about 10 minutes. Pour in the hot stock, bring to the boil and simmer steadily for 20 minutes, when the vegetables should be very soft. Liquidise and push through a sieve into the rinsed out pan. Stir in the cream and adjust the seasoning. Serve hot, in warmed bowls, garnished with dill sprigs.

FOUR SERVINGS

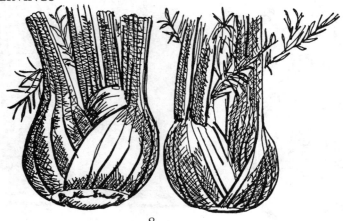

BUTTERNUT SQUASH & PEAR SOUP

The mellow sweetness of the squash is perfectly enhanced by the fragrance of pears. Quintessentially autumnal flavours captured by Anna Thomas in *From Anna's Kitchen*.

1½lb/750g butternut squash, peeled, seeded and chopped
3 ripe pears
2 onions, peeled and chopped
1½oz/3 tbsp/45g butter
1¾ pints/4 cups/1 litre boiling chicken or vegetable stock
salt and pepper
2 tbsp chopped coriander/cilantro and 4 tbsp crème fraîche to garnish

Melt the butter and stew the onion with a good pinch of salt for about 10 minutes until they are very soft. Peel, halve, core and slice the pears and add to the onions with the squash. Cover the pan and continue to cook slowly until meltingly soft and buttery, another 10 minutes. Pour in the boiling stock, bring to the boil and simmer steadily until the vegetables are nicely tender, about 20 minutes. Liquidise and push through a sieve into the rinsed out pan. Reheat, adjust the seasoning and serve in warmed bowls with a spoonful of crème fraîche and a sprinkling of coriander.

FOUR SERVINGS

Chilled Avocado Soup
with Tomato Salsa

You have two choices of how to proceed in making this recipe from Annie Bell's *More Taste Than Time*. Either, make just before serving with well-chilled ingredients. Or, make it a few hours before serving, bury the stones in the soup, press cling film well into surface to seal it from all air and put it in the fridge to chill; but do be prepared to scoop off just a top layer of brown and you will find the soup will be bright and green underneath.

for the salsa
10oz/300g ripe plum tomatoes
2 tbsp olive oil
salt, pepper and a pinch of sugar
1 tsp soy sauce
1 tsp lime juice
1 tbsp finely chopped coriander/cilantro

for the soup
4 ripe, firm avocados
1 lemon grass stalk
2 spring onions, chopped
juice of 2 limes
5fl oz/⅔ cup/150ml double cream
½ pint/1¼ cups/300ml milk
12fl oz/2½ cups/360ml vegetable stock
salt and pepper

First make the salsa. Cut out the stem end of the tomatoes with a small, sharp knife. Peel the tomatoes by putting in a bowl, pouring over boiling water to cover and leaving for a minute: their skins should slip off easily. Cut in half, scoop out the seeds with a teaspoon and dice evenly. Mix well with the rest of the salsa ingredients.

For the soup, trim the lemon grass, strip away the tough outer leaves and finely chop the tender inner stalk. Halve, stone and peel the avocados. Put all the ingredients in a food processor and work until smooth. Serve chilled, and garnished with a spoonful of salsa.

FOUR SERVINGS

SWEET ONION & ROSEMARY SOUP
WITH STILTON TOASTS

A very very delicious winter soup, utilising that classic soup partnership of onion and cheese, from Jennifer Paterson and Clarissa Dickson Wright's *Two Fat Ladies*.

8 onions, peeled and chopped
4oz/8 tbsp/120g butter
1 sprig of rosemary, leaves stripped and finely chopped
salt and pepper
1¾ pints/4 cups/1 litre boiling chicken or vegetable stock
4oz/120g Stilton
8 slices of French stick

Melt the butter, stir in the onions, rosemary and a good pinch of salt and stew slowly, with the lid on, for 20 minutes, until the onions are very soft and buttery yellow. Pour in the hot stock, bring to the boil and leave to bubble away quite vigorously for half an hour.

Lightly toast the bread until crisp and pale gold, and spread thickly with Stilton cheese. Give the soup a final seasoning, then ladle into warmed bowls and float the toasts on top.

FOUR SERVINGS

Tuscan Chickpea & Tomato Soup
with Pancetta & Sage

A warming, rustic soup from Rena Salaman's *Healthy Mediterranean Cooking*. It is easily vegetarianised, just omit the pancetta, and if you don't have sage, rosemary is perfect too.

> 7oz/210g dried chickpeas, soaked overnight and cooked
> for 1½ hours until tender, or 14oz/400g tin of
> chickpeas, drained and rinsed
> 3 tbsp olive oil
> 1 onion, peeled and chopped
> 4 garlic cloves, peeled and sliced
> 2 celery sticks, chopped
> 4oz/120g pancetta, diced
> 6 sage leaves
> 14oz/400g tin of peeled chopped Italian plum tomatoes
> 1¾ pints/4 cups/1 litre boiling chicken, vegetable or
> chickpea stock
> salt and pepper

Warm the oil and add the onion, garlic, celery, pancetta and sage. Cook, stirring very often, until the vegetables are very soft and pale gold, about 15 minutes. Add the tomatoes, chickpeas and seasoning, stir well, and leave to stew for another 10 minutes before pouring in the boiling stock. Cook the soup at a gentle, steady boil for 15 minutes. Correct the seasoning with salt, pepper, and maybe a drop of vinegar or pinch of sugar. Ladle into warmed bowls; if you have some extra special delicious olive oil to hand, you may like to swirl just a little over the soup.

FOUR SERVINGS

CORN SOUP WITH RED PEPPER PURÉE

A stunning soup, colour and flavour-wise, from Alice Waters' *Chez Panisse Vegetables*. The pepper purée makes a red centre in the yellow soup and its smoky heat perfectly compliments the natural sweetness of the corn. We owe the discovery of this recipe to Lindsay Bonner, a South African cook and newcomer to the Books for Cooks Kitchen. She has an overiding passion for sweetcorn soups.

for the soup
4 cobs of corn, kernels stripped with a sharp knife
1oz/2 tbsp/30g butter
1 onion, peeled and chopped
2 garlic cloves, peeled and chopped
1 leek, white parts only, chopped
½ carrot, peeled and chopped
1¼ pints/3 cups/750ml boiling chicken or vegetable stock
4 tbsp double/heavy cream
salt, pepper, lemon juice, sugar

for the purée
2 red peppers, quartered and seeded
a smidgen of garlic, crushed
salt, pepper, Tabasco

Put the pepper quarters skin side up under a hot grill and cook until charred and blistered all over. Now put them in a bowl, cover with a tea towel, and leave for 10 minutes while the trapped steam loosens the pepper skins so they may easily be slipped off. Put the peeled peppers into a blender or food processor with a tiny bit of crushed garlic and a few tablespoons of the stock for the soup and work to a purée. Push through a sieve for absolute smoothness and correct the seasoning.

Melt the butter and stew the onion, garlic, carrot and leek with a large pinch of salt and the lid on until soft and wilted, about 15 minutes. Pour in the hot stock and simmer for another 5 to 10 minutes to finish cooking the vegetables. Now add the corn, bring back to a rolling boil, and turn off the heat at once. Cover and leave for about 3 minutes before puréeing the soup very thoroughly in a blender or food processor — leave it whizzing for at least 3 minutes. Push the soup through a sieve into the rinsed out pan, stir in the cream, thin if necessary and correct the seasoning. Ladle the hot soup into warmed bowls and spoon the red pepper purée into the middle of each soup. Serve at once.

FOUR SERVINGS

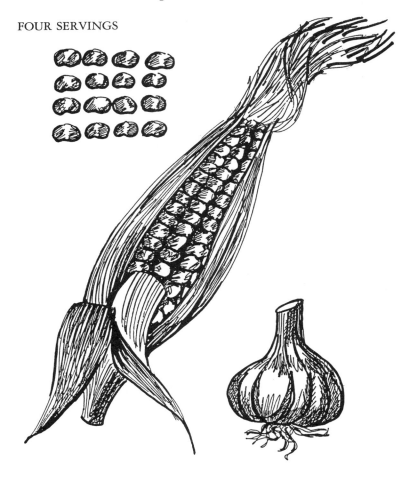

PROVENCAL WINTER VEGETABLE SOUP
WITH PARSLEY PISTOU

From Patricia Wells' *At Home in Provence*. Certainly in its native Nice, *pistou* is made with basil, but then parsley flourishes throughout much of the winter and is thus a more appropriate partner for the winter roots which feature in this soup. *Pistou* freezes very well; clever, far-sighted people will buy and nurture cheap basil plants all through the summer and make a winter store for their freezers to cheer up darker months with the quintessentially summer flavour of basil.

1 leek, white and tender green parts only, finely sliced
4 celery sticks, finely sliced
1 onion, peeled, halved and finely sliced
2 garlic cloves, peeled and finely sliced
4 tbsp olive oil
salt and pepper
2 carrots, peeled, halved and sliced
8oz/240g potatoes, peeled and cubed
14oz/200g tin of whole Italian plum tomatoes
2 turnips, peeled and cubed
7oz/210g dried white beans, soaked overnight and
cooked for 1½ hours until tender, or 14oz/400g tin
of white beans, drained and rinsed
bouquet garni of 2 bay leaves and 3 thyme sprigs
1¾ pint/4 cups/1 litre boiling chicken or vegetable stock
1 nest of vermicelli (angel's hair pasta), broken into small pieces
4oz/1 cup/125g Gruyère, grated

for the pistou
2 garlic cloves, peeled and chopped
salt
a handful of flat-leaf parsley, chopped
8 tbsp olive oil

Warm the oil and stir in the leek, celery, onion and garlic with a large pinch of salt. Stew slowly, covered, stirring frequently, until softened, about 10 minutes. Add the rest of the vegetables and the herbs, stir well and cook for 5 minutes. Pour in the hot stock, bring to the boil and simmer steadily for half an hour.

While the soup is bubbling away, make the *pistou*. Put the garlic and salt in a mortar and pound with a pestle until smooth. Still pounding, add the parsley little by little and work to a bright green paste. Add the oil drop by drop at first, and then more quickly, stirring until you have a thick sauce. This can of course all be done in a blender or food processor speedily and effortlessly, as long as you have someone else on hand to wash and dry up.

About 10 minutes before the soup is required, add the pasta and boil until cooked. Adjust the seasoning and serve in warmed bowls, garnished generously with Gruyère cheese and parsley *pistou*.

NOTE   *Pistou* keeps well, covered and chilled, for a few days, or frozen for up to 6 months. Make sure you bring it right up to room temperature and stir vigorously before serving.

FOUR SERVINGS

CURRIED DAHL SOUP WITH CORIANDER YOGHURT

A good-looking and good-tasting soup coloured and curried yellow with aromatic Indian spices and served with a refreshing herb-yoghurt garnish. From *Blakes* by Andrew Blake.

7oz/210g dried chickpeas, soaked overnight and cooked
for 1½ hours until tender, or 14oz/400g tin of
chickpeas, drained and rinsed
1 onion, peeled and chopped
2 garlic cloves, peeled and chopped
2 tbsp sunflower oil
1 tbsp turmeric
1 tbsp ground cumin
1 tbsp brown mustard seeds
6 curry leaves
1¼ pints/3 cups/750ml boiling chicken or vegetable stock
8fl oz/240ml coconut milk
a handful of coriander/cilantro, very finely chopped
5fl oz/⅔ cup/150ml thick creamy yoghurt
salt and pepper

Warm the oil and fry the onion with a pinch of salt over a moderate flame, stirring often, until soft and yellow, about 10 minutes. Add the garlic and spices and fry for another 5 minutes until golden and aromatic. Tip in the chickpeas, stir well and leave for a couple of minutes to infuse the garlicky spices. Pour in the boiling stock and simmer for 15 minutes.

While the soup is cooking, make the garnish by mixing the coriander with the yoghurt. Liquidise the dahl and broth until smooth with the coconut milk, return to the rinsed out pan, reheat and adjust the seasoning. Ladle into warmed bowls and drop a large spoonful of coriander yoghurt into the centre of the soup.

FOUR SERVINGS

Main Courses

HONEY-GLAZED DUCK
WITH GRAPEFRUIT & GINGER SALAD

Our in-house artist and illustrator of these books, Selina Snow, recently moved to Australia, much to our collective chagrin. To give her a good send off, we drove down to Wiltshire to spend a jolly 24 hours with Victoria. When we arrived, cold and hungry, we were greeted by the delicious aroma of this duck salad (adapted from Jennifer Paterson and Clarissa Dickson Wright's *Two Fat Ladies*). Victoria served it on a large platter (instead of portioned plates) with the duck fanned out decoratively on a bed of salad leaves and the warm grapefruit and ginger dressing spooned over. We strongly advise you to do the same. A special dish for special times.

4 duck breasts
1 tbsp runny honey
1 tbsp dark soy sauce

for the salad
2 pink grapefruit
2oz/60g caster/granulated sugar
2 tbsp runny honey
2 tbsp dark soy sauce
juice of 1 lemon
1 inch/2½cm fresh root ginger, peeled and finely chopped
salt and pepper
4 handfuls of young spinach and chicory/Belgian endive leaves

Score the skin of the duck breasts in a cross-hatch pattern. Stir the honey and soy together and roll duck breasts in this mixture.

Cut a slice from each end of the grapefruits and stand it upright on the chopping board. With a sharp knife, cut away the peel, working from top to bottom, following the curve of the fruit, and removing as much of the white pith and skin as possible. Cut the peeled grapefruit into segments, carefully slicing in between the skin and working over a bowl to catch all the juice. Squeeze the skin, pith and pulp in your hands to extract as much juice as possible.

Put the sugar in a pan over a moderate flame and heat until the sugar dissolves and cooks to a light caramel, shaking the pan to swirl the sugar so that it colours evenly. Take off the heat and pour in the grapefruit juice, standing well back as the cold juice splutters and splatters when it hits the boiling caramel. Put the pan back on the heat and stir until the caramel dissolves into the juice. Add the honey, soy, lemon, ginger and grapefruit segments, correct the seasoning and keep warm over a gentle flame.

Heat the oven to 190C/375F/Gas 5. Heat a heavy frying pan over a moderate flame, and, when it is hot, put in the duck breasts, skin side down, and cook for about 5 minutes, until the fat has melted and the skin browned. Pour off the fat, turn the breasts over and put into the oven to roast for 10 minutes, when they should still be pink, or 12 minutes for *à point*. Test them with the point of a knife to check. Take them out of the pan and let them rest (either wrapped in foil or on a dish in the turned off oven with the door slightly open) for 5 minutes. Then slice each duck breast across on the diagonal and serve at once with the salad leaves and warm grapefruit-ginger dressing.

NOTE   The dressing can certainly be prepared the day before and warmed gently just before serving.

FOUR SERVINGS

CHICKEN STEWED IN SAFFRON & FENNEL
WITH RED PEPPER AIOLI

A fabulous re-working of that legendary Provençal dish, *bouillabaisse*, which is near impossible to reproduce at home since the correct Mediterranean fish for an authentic rendition can simply not be bought away from those shores. So Patricia Wells forgets the fish but keeps the sunny flavours of fennel, garlic and saffron to create this glorious stew. From *At Home in Provence*.

for the stew
8 chicken thighs, skinned, boned and cut in half
salt and pepper
3 tbsp olive oil
2 garlic cloves, peeled and finely chopped
a pinch of saffron threads, or ½ tsp saffron powder,
infused in 1 tbsp hot water
1 tsp fennel seeds
3 sprigs of thyme
4 fresh or 2 dry bay leaves
2 tbsp tomato purée
2 tbsp pastis liqueur (such as Pernod or Ricard)
8fl oz/1 cup/240ml dry white wine
16fl oz/2 cups/480ml chicken stock
1lb/500g potatoes, peeled and quartered lengthwise

for the aioli
1 red pepper, quartered
6 garlic cloves, peeled and chopped
½ tsp salt
2 free-range egg yolks, at room temperature
8fl oz/1 cup/240ml olive oil
¼ tsp cayenne pepper

Season the chicken pieces with salt and pepper. Warm the oil and cook the chicken until golden on both sides. Take the chicken out of the pan and add the garlic, spices, herbs, purée, liqueur, wine and stock and bring to the boil. Add the chicken and potatoes and simmer slowly until cooked, about 20 minutes.

While the stew is simmering, make the *aioli*. Put the pepper quarters skin side up under a hot grill and cook until charred and blistered all over. Now put them in a bowl, cover with a tea towel, and leave for 10 minutes while the trapped steam loosens the pepper skins so they may easily be slipped off. You can use either a pestle and mortar or a food processor. If using the machine, put the pepper quarters in a food processor with the garlic, salt and egg yolks and work to a paste. Trickle in the oil slowly until the mixture thickens to mayonnaise. If working by hand, first chop the pepper, then pound to a purée with the garlic and salt, then mix in the egg yolks and work in the oil, drop by drop until thick. Season with cayenne pepper.

Serve hot in warmed bowls garnished with generous spoonfuls of the red pepper *aioli*.

FOUR SERVINGS

SMOKED SALMON & LENTIL SALAD
WITH WALNUT VINAIGRETTE

Puy lentils are a tiny mottled green variety with a good earthy flavour from the Auvergne, a mountainous region bang in the middle of France. They are very much preferred when making salads because of their ability to hold their shape when cooked (turn to page 70 for Puy Lentils with Dill, Salsa Verde and Roast Peppers). A fabulous fusion of flavours from David Rosengarten's *Dean & Deluca Cookbook*.

12oz/1½ cups/360g Puy lentils, rinsed
salt and pepper
4 rashers of streaky bacon, fried till very crisp and crumbled
5oz/150g smoked salmon slices
a handful of fresh dill, finely chopped
2 heads of chicory/Belgian endive, leaves separated
4 tbsp sour cream
lots of dill sprigs to garnish

for the vinaigrette
2 shallots, peeled and finely chopped
4 tbsp red wine vinegar
1 tbsp Dijon mustard
4fl oz/½ cup/120ml walnut oil

Rinse the lentils, put in a pan, cover generously with water, bring to the boil and simmer slowly until the lentils are tender — which will take anything from 20 to 40 minutes, depending on that unknown quantity, how old they are. Keep an eye on them because although you want them to be cooked, you also want them to be whole rather than pottage. While the lentils are cooking make the vinaigrette by putting all the ingredients in a jam jar and shaking well until smooth and emulsified. Drain the cooked lentils of all liquid, pour over about two-thirds of the vinaigrette (without stirring which might crush the hot lentils) and leave to cool slightly.

Cut the salmon slices into strips about 4 inches/10cm long and 2 inches/5cm wide. Mix the chopped dill into the lentils and correct the seasoning. Dress the chicory leaves with most of the remaining vinaigrette and arrange them like flowers on each plate. Mound the lentils on the bed of chicory, scatter with the crispy bacon pieces and drape over the salmon strips. Top with a spoonful of sour cream, spoon around the rest of the dressing, grind over black pepper and decorate with masses of dill sprigs.

NOTE   This salad is at its best eaten when the lentils are still just warm, but they can be cooked and dressed and kept covered and chilled for up to a week before assembling the salad with the salmon et cetera — but do be sure to bring them back to room temperature before serving.

FOUR SERVINGS

Wild Mushroom & Mascarpone Tart
with Basil

A gorgeous tart, deeply and richly flavoured, from Ursula's *Real Fast Vegetarian*. If you can't find mascarpone, Ursula suggests sour cream instead. Don't restrict yourself to basil either; chopped parsley, thyme or rosemary are good too.

½oz/¾ cup/15g dried porcini
12oz/360g mushrooms, sliced (use some wild ones if you can,
or cultivated brown, field/portobello, oyster or shiitake,
or a mixture)
2oz/4 tbsp/60g butter
1 onion, peeled and finely chopped
1 garlic clove, peeled and finely chopped
salt and pepper
3 free-range eggs, beaten
8oz/1 cup/250g mascarpone
2oz/60g Parmesan, grated
a handful of fresh basil, sliced
9½ inch/24cm shortcrust pastry case baked
blind/pre-baked
(see pages 122-4)

Soak the dried porcini in hand-hot water for about half an hour, then lift them out, squeeze as much water as possible out of them and chop finely. (Strain the soaking liquid through kitchen paper and use for stock-making).

Put a baking tray into the oven and heat to 180C/350F/Gas 4. Melt the butter and soften the onion and garlic with a pinch of salt, then add the mushrooms and stir-fry over quite a high heat until they absorb their juices and begin to brown, about 5 minutes. Correct the seasoning and cool slightly. Beat the eggs and mascarpone until smooth (you might want to use a whisk for this as the mascarpone is very thick) and stir in the cheese, herbs and mushrooms. Pour the mushroom-mascarpone mixture into the pastry case and put into the oven on to the hot baking tray (a good tactic to avert soggy pastry bottoms) and cook until set to a quite beautiful golden brown, about 30-40 minutes. Serve warm rather than hot, with a simple green leaf salad dressed with lemon juice, olive oil and grated Parmesan.

FOUR SERVINGS

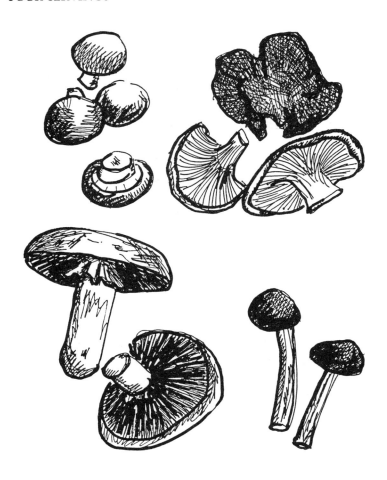

VICTORIA'S MARINATED FILLET OF LAMB WITH CORIANDER-YOGHURT SAUCE

This recipe of Victoria's is rather special, slightly extravagant but truly delicious, so try it.

for the lamb
1½lb/750g lamb fillet (not the inexpensive neck fillet,
if your butcher doesn't know what you mean ask for the
eye of the loin)
1 tsp cumin seeds
salt and pepper
1 tbsp olive oil
2 garlic cloves, peeled and crushed
4 handfuls of young spinach leaves
a handful of fresh herbs (parsley, thyme, oregano)
2 tbsp pine nuts, toasted

for the sauce
2 heads of garlic
1 tbsp olive oil
5 fl oz/⅔ cup/150ml thick creamy yoghurt
2 tbsp double/heavy cream
1 tsp Dijon mustard
2 tbsp balsamic vinegar
½ tsp cumin seeds
1 tsp coriander seeds
salt, pepper and freshly grated nutmeg

Rub the lamb all over with the cumin, oil and garlic, cover well and leave to marinate for several hours or overnight in the fridge.

To make the sauce, start by roasting the garlic. Heat the oven to 180C/350F/Gas 4. Slice off the top quarter of the garlic bulb to expose the cloves. Put the garlic on a piece of foil, sprinkle with the olive oil, salt and pepper, wrap up and bake for 45 minutes. Take out of the oven and cool slightly before squeezing out the garlic pulp from the papery skins. Put the roasted garlic pulp with the rest of the sauce ingredients in a food processor and work to a purée. Correct the seasoning.

Turn the oven up to 220C/425F/Gas 7. Sprinkle the marinated lamb with salt and pepper and brown well on all sides in a little oil in a hot pan. Put into the oven to roast for 12-15 minutes. Wrap up the fillet in foil and let it rest for 10 minutes.

To serve, divide the spinach and herbs between each plate, heaping them up nicely. Slice the lamb, arrange it over the spinach, pour over the sauce and scatter with pine nuts. Victoria likes to serve this with crispy herb-roasted potatoes (look back to our second book for Potatoes Roasted with Lemon and Rosemary).

NOTE   The sauce can certainly be prepared ahead of time. If you want to serve the sauce hot, either you must heat it gently through without boiling, or you must first stabilise the yoghurt so it doesn't curdle. To stabilise, stir 1 teaspoon of cornflour mixed to a paste with a little water into the yoghurt sauce and bring to the boil, stirring all the time. Simmer gently, uncovered, for a couple of minutes to cook the starch. Stir in the lamb juices and serve.

FOUR SERVINGS

GARLIC & GOAT'S CHEESE CUSTARDS
WITH GRILLED TOMATO SAUCE

These herb-scented, velvet-textured creams, with their mellow garlic and mild goat's cheese flavour, come from Stephanie Alexander's *The Cook's Companion*.

for the sauce
8 ripe tomatoes
salt, pepper and sugar
olive oil
balsamic vinegar

for the custards
12 garlic cloves
½ pint/1¼ cups/300 ml milk
1 bay leaf
1 thyme sprig
4oz/120g fresh rindless goat's cheese
2 free-range eggs, beaten
salt and pepper (preferably white)
freshly grated nutmeg
¼ pint/⅔ cup/150ml double/heavy cream, chilled
(this is important)

Cut the tomatoes in half and scoop out the seeds with a teaspoon. Put them cut side up on a roasting dish, sprinkle with a little salt, pepper, sugar and oil and cook under a hot grill (very close to the heat) until softened and slightly charred, 5-10 minutes.

Heat the oven to 160C/325F/Gas 3 and butter 4 individual ramekins. Put the garlic cloves in a pan, cover with cold water, bring to the boil, and simmer gently for about a minute. Drain, cover with fresh water, boil, simmer and drain again. Now cook the garlic cloves in the milk with the herbs for about 10 minutes, or until completely soft. Let the milk cool completely. When the milk is cold, fish out the herbs and purée the garlic and milk with the goat's cheese and eggs in a food processor until smooth. Pour in the chilled cream and, using the pulse button, beat in until well-mixed. Do not overbeat. Correct the seasoning before pouring into the ramekins. Stand the ramekins on a tea towel or piece of newspaper in a roasting dish and pour in boiling water to come halfway up the sides of the ramekins. Put into the oven and cook for about 25-35 minutes or until set and firm to the touch.

When they are done let them cool slightly (about 10-15 minutes) while you warm through the grilled tomato sauce, letting it bubble away until slightly thickened. Run a sharp knife around the edges of the custards and unmould them on to warmed plates. Correct the seasoning of the sauce and add a splash of balsamic vinegar before spooning on top of the custards. Serve at once, with a rocket (arugula) salad and warm bread.

NOTE   The custards can be made the day before and served hot the next day. Do not unmould them and let them cool completely before covering with cling film and chilling. Reheat in a microwave, or a hot water filled roasting dish *(bain-marie)* in a 160C/325F/Gas 3 oven for 15-20 minutes.

FOUR SERVINGS

PORK FILLET IN GINGER BEER SAUCE

Great British Grub with Great British Flavours. From Michael Driver and Jenny Linford's *The Tate Cookbook.*

1lb/500g pork fillet/tenderloin, trimmed
2 tbsp flour
1oz/1 tbsp/30g butter
2 tbsp olive oil
1 onion, peeled and finely chopped
1 garlic clove, peeled and finely chopped
½ inch/1cm piece of fresh root ginger, peeled and finely chopped
1 celery stick, cut into matchsticks
1 carrot, peeled and cut into matchsticks
1 parsnip, peeled and cut into matchsticks
6fl oz/¾ cup/180ml ginger beer
4fl oz/½ cup/120ml chicken or vegetable stock
4 sprigs of thyme, leaves stripped
a handful of coriander/cilantro, finely chopped
4 tbsp thick creamy yoghurt

Cut the fillet into ½ inch/1cm thick slices on the diagonal. Lightly dust the pork with the flour and season with pepper. Melt the butter with the oil in a frying pan and, when it is hot, add the pork to the pan and fry until brown and crispy on both sides. Take the pork slices out of the pan and stir in the onion, garlic and ginger and fry until fragrant and slightly softened, about 3 minutes. Add the celery, carrot and parsnip strips and cook for another 3 minutes. Pour in the ginger beer, stock, thyme and 2 tbsp of the coriander. Bring to the boil and simmer steadily until the liquid is reduced by two thirds and the vegetables are tender, about 10 minutes. Put the pork back into the sauce, stir well and simmer for another 5 minutes or until cooked through. Stir in the yoghurt and the rest of the coriander and serve at once with Jennifer's Roasted Garlic Potato Purée (see page 44).

FOUR SERVINGS

CELIA'S CREAMY MADEIRA MUSHROOMS
WITH APPLE

This clever concoction of Celia's is as versatile as it is delicious; try it as a topping for crostini, a filling for pancakes or (our favourite) as a warm salad on a bed of crisp salad leaves. It has the added benefit of taking a mere matter of minutes to prepare.

2 Granny Smith apples
juice of 1 lemon
14oz/400g selection of wild mushrooms, thickly sliced (especially chanterelles and ceps but cultivated brown, field/portobello, oyster or shiitake mushrooms will do)
1 glass of Madeira wine
5oz/⅔ cup/150g mascarpone
1oz/2 tbsp/30g butter
salt and pepper
parsley sprigs to garnish

Peel, quarter, core and slice the apples; toss the slices very well in the lemon juice, both to season and discourage discolouration. Melt the butter over a moderate heat in a large frying pan and stir in the mushrooms. When they have soaked up the butter and started to soften, add the apple slices and stir fry for a couple of minutes. Pour in the Madiera and cook, stirring until it has almost bubbled away entirely and the juices are beginning to caramelise. Now add in the mascarpone and stir until the mushrooms and apples are evenly coated in the sweet and creamy sauce. Correct the seasoning and serve hot, garnished with sprigs of parsley.

FOUR SERVINGS

LAMB BRAISED IN RED WINE WITH ROOT VEGETABLES & ROSEMARY GREMOLADA

David Rosengarten, in his *The Dean & Deluca Cookbook,* re-styles a lamb stew after the Milanese superdish *osso buco,* taking its traditional garnish, *gremolada,* and swapping parsley and lemon for rosemary and orange, and adding a few other contemporary touches of his own. The classic accompaniment to *osso buco* is of course saffron risotto; while David Rosengarten suggests creamy polenta, we rather favour saffron-tinted and flavoured mashed potatoes (see page 82).

for the braise
4 lamb shanks or 2lb/1kg lamb shoulder, fat trimmed
and cut into 2 inch/5cm pieces
3 tbsp olive oil
salt and pepper
2 onions, peeled and chopped
4 carrots, peeled and diced
3 fresh rosemary sprigs
2 bay leaves
4 garlic cloves, peeled and chopped
16fl oz/2 cups/500 ml red wine
1lb/500g parsnips, peeled and diced

for the gremolada
4 rosemary sprigs, leaves stripped
grated zest of 1 orange
1 garlic clove, peeled and chopped

Warm the oil in a heavy pan (which must have a close-fitting lid) over a moderate flame. When it is hot, sear the lamb pieces; put only a few at a time in the pan (too many and they will steam rather than fry) and brown them rapidly but thoroughly on all sides. Put the pieces aside when done, sprinkle with salt and pepper, and carry on till all the lamb is browned and out of the pan.

Throw the onions, carrots and herbs into the pan and stir-fry until the onions are quite soft and catching a little around the edges. Pour in the wine and bring to a fierce boil, vigorously scraping the bottom of the pan to dissolve all the crusty caramelised juices. Bubble away for 5 minutes, then turn down the heat to a bare simmer and stir in the lamb. Cover the pan first with a piece of foil and then with a lid and cook very slowly over a mere flicker of a flame for 1½ hours. Then add the diced parsnips, put the lid back on and cook for a final half an hour.

While the parsnips are cooking, make the gremolada by chopping finely together the rosemary, orange zest and garlic. Sprinkle the wine-braised lamb and roots with the gremolada just before serving, and accompany with the creamy starchy side dish of your choice.

NOTE   All braises, daubes and stews are better still cooked a day before, and this one is no exception.

FOUR SERVINGS

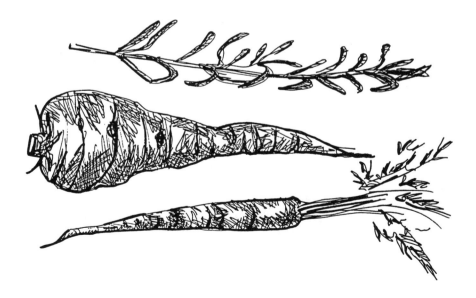

35

CHICKEN & PAPAYA SALAD
WITH POMEGRANATE DRESSING

An exotic rendition of that old favourite, chicken salad, from Julie Sahni's *Savoring Spices and Herbs*. It is open to some adaptation: you can use mango which is rather more widely available than papaya, and pine nuts if you prefer them to walnuts as Victoria does. It makes a splendid summer buffet centrepiece on a platter lined with decoratively different salad leaves. Do seek out pomegranate syrup (molasses) at The Spice Shop (see page 126) or in Lebanese and Iranian shops, where you can also buy pomegranates all year round, so you can finish the salad with a scattering of their jewel-like seeds.

4 chicken breasts, boned and skinned
1 onion, peeled and quartered
a few bay leaves
5 black peppercorns and a pinch of salt
2 carrots, peeled
3oz/90g walnut pieces
1 ripe papaya, peeled, seeded and diced
1 large or 2 small heads of radicchio
coriander/cilantro sprigs to garnish

for the dressing
6 tbsp pomegranate syrup/molasses
4 tbsp orange juice
8 tbsp olive oil
1 inch/2.5cm piece of root ginger, peeled and finely chopped
1 garlic clove, peeled and finely chopped
1 red onion, peeled and finely chopped
a handful of coriander/cilantro, finely chopped
1 fresh green chilli, seeded and finely chopped
1 tsp cumin seeds, toasted and crushed
salt

Poach the chicken: put in a pan with the onion quarters, bay leaves and seasoning, cover with cold water, bring slowly to the boil and cook in barely simmering water for 15 minutes. Turn off the heat and let the chicken cool in its poaching liquid. Cut the cooled chicken into ½ inch/1cm dice.

Make the dressing by mixing together all the ingredients into a large bowl and leave to macerate until you are ready to eat. Cut the carrots into fine matchstick strips *(julienne)*. Bring a pan of water to a rolling boil, tip in the carrot sticks and, when the water comes back to the boil, drain and refresh under cold running water. This blanching and refreshing preserves the colour, texture and flavour of the carrots.

Toast the walnut pieces in a dry pan over a slow heat until lightly coloured and nuttily aromatic. Carefully separate the radicchio leaves and choose the 12 largest leaves to serve the salad on. Stack the rest of the leaves one on top of another, roll tightly up and slice across the roll into fine strips.

Just before serving stir the chicken, about half the carrot sticks, the walnuts, and sliced radicchio into the bowl with the dressing and mix carefully so that all the ingredients are well dressed. Arrange 3 radicchio leaves like a red flower on each plate and heap the salad in the middle. Top with the rest of the carrot sticks and garnish with coriander sprigs. Serve at once.

NOTE   You can certainly poach the chicken the day before; let it cool in its poaching liquid and keep covered and chilled. Or you could use leftover roast chicken. You can prepare all the salad ingredients, make the dressing and keep separately, covered and chilled until required up to 3 hours in advance. Then assemble and dress the salad when you are ready to eat.

FOUR SERVINGS

COURGETTE FRITTERS WITH RADISH TZATZIKI

These fritters with their uniquely fresh and fragrant citrus flavour come from Alice Waters' *Chez Panisse Vegetables*. We love the contrast of the hot, green and gold fritters and the cold, pink and white sauce, and hope you do, too.

for the fritters
1½lb/750g courgettes/zucchini, trimmed
salt, pepper and freshly grated nutmeg
1 garlic clove, peeled and finely chopped
a handful of chives, chopped
1 tbsp thyme leaves
grated zest of 3 lemons
1 tbsp cornflour
1 free-range egg and 1 yolk, beaten

for the tzatziki
6 red radishes, trimmed and grated
1 red onion, peeled and finely chopped
1 garlic clove, peeled and finely chopped
a handful of mint, finely chopped
2 tbsp lemon juice
1 tbsp olive oil
5fl oz/⅔ cup/150ml thick creamy yoghurt
salt and pepper

oil for frying
4 handfuls of lightly dressed salad leaves to serve
lemon wedges and mint sprigs to decorate

Grate the courgettes, put them in a colander and sprinkle them with 1 tsp salt. Leave them for half an hour to degorge.

Meanwhile make the tzatziki by mixing all the ingredients together and correct the seasoning.

After half an hour, squeeze as much water out of the courgettes as you can with your hands, then wrap them up in a tea towel and wring out the rest of the water — you'll be amazed at how much liquid they produce. Put the courgettes in a large bowl and mix well with the rest of the fritter ingredients.

Heat a couple of tablespoons of oil in non-stick frying pan over a moderate heat. When it is hot pile 2 tbsp of courgette batter for each fritter in the pan and flatten to a 4 inch/10cm round and fry for several minutes, without prodding or poking, when they should be crisp and golden underneath and firm enough to turn over. Then cook on the other side until that is nicely coloured too. Keep hot in the oven on a baking tray while you cook the rest of the fritters, oiling the pan between batches.

Divide the salad leaves between 4 plates, arrange the hot courgette fritters on top, spoon over the radish tzatziki and serve with a wedge of lemon and a mint sprig.

NOTE   The fritter batter can be prepared several hours in advance and kept coverered and chilled until you are ready to cook. The tzatziki, however, can be made the day before and kept covered and chilled.

FOUR SERVINGS

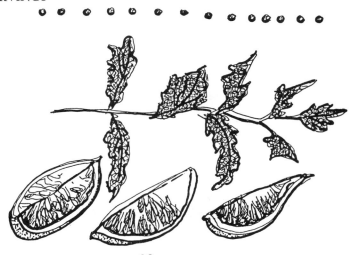

MILDLY SPICED CARAMELISED ONION TARTLETS OF HAZELNUT PASTRY WITH TOMATO & BASIL SAUCE

The tartlets require four 4 inch/10cm tart tins, but exactly the same quantities given in this recipe line and fill a 9½ inch/24cm tart tin. The hazelnut pastry is a little temperamental, and a novice pastry maker might do better to turn to page 122 and make our shortcrust pastry, adding a tablespoon of ground hazelnuts. The ground ginger, malt vinegar and Barbados sugar are tremendously English flavours; their combination in these very special onion tartlets comes from Michael Driver and Jenny Linford's *The Tate Cookbook*.

for the pastry
6oz/1½ cups/180g plain/all-purpose flour, sifted
2oz/½ cup/60g ground hazelnuts (see note below)
a good pinch of salt
3oz/¾ stick/90g very cold butter, cubed
1 free-range egg yolk and 1 tbsp cold water

for the filling
6 onions, peeled, halved and finely sliced
2 garlic cloves peeled and finely chopped
2oz/½ stick/60g butter
3oz/6 tbsp/90g dark brown sugar
6 tbsp malt vinegar
a handful coriander, finely chopped
1½ tsp ground ginger
8fl oz/1 cup/240ml milk
3 free-range eggs, beaten

for the sauce
1 onion, peeled and finely chopped
1 garlic clove, peeled and finely chopped

1lb/500g ripe fresh tomatoes, or 14oz/400g tin of
chopped Italian plum tomatoes and 2 tsp tomato purée
2 tbsp olive oil
salt and pepper
a handful of basil, finely sliced

First make the pastry. Lightly butter four 4 inch/10cm tartlet tins or one 9½ inch/24cm tart tin and put it into the refrigerator. Put the flour, ground nuts and salt in a food processor and aerate with a couple of quick on/off pulses. Add the butter and process till the mixture resembles fine breadcrumbs. Add the yolk and water (if needed) and process until the pastry just draws together. Turn it out on to a lightly floured work surface and knead briefly to form a flat round. (If you don't have a food processor, do the whole thing as lightly as possible, using your fingertips to rub the butter into the flour-nut mixture and, when you add the liquid, pinching the whole thing into a dough.) Wrap the pastry tightly in cling film and chill in the refrigerator for 30 minutes or until it is firm. Roll the chilled pastry out and line the tartlet tins, trimming the edges with a generous hand as the pastry might shrink. Put them into the refrigerator to rest for at least an hour, or into the freezer for 15 minutes, if you're pushed for time.

While the pastry is resting, make the filling and sauce. Melt the butter and soften the onions with the lid on for 5 minutes, then uncover and fry until lightly golden. Stir in the garlic, sugar, vinegar, coriander and ginger and cook quickly until all the vinegar has bubbled away, about 10 minutes. Turn off the heat and adjust the seasoning. Beat together the milk and eggs.

Make the sauce. If you are using fresh ripe tomatoes, cut out their core end with a small knife and put them in a bowl. Pour over boiling water to cover and leave for a minute, when the skins should peel off easily. Cut the peeled tomatoes in half, scoop out the seeds with a teaspoon and roughly chop them. Warm the oil and soften the onion and garlic with a good pinch of salt. Stir in the chopped tomatoes and tomato purée, raise the heat and cook hard for 15 minutes, if the tomatoes are fresh, or more slowly for 30 minutes, if they are tinned. Season with salt, pepper, basil and perhaps a pinch of sugar.

Put a baking tray in the oven and heat to 190C/375F/Gas 5 (having a hot baking tray in the oven helps the pastry case cook more evenly, otherwise the sides tend to cook before the base). Line the chilled pastry cases with baking parchment, fill with baking beans and cook for 10 minutes. Carefully remove the paper and beans and cook for another 10 minutes or a little longer, until a light biscuit brown. Spread the caramelised onions in an even layer over the bottoms of the tartlets, pour over the milk-egg custard and put the filled tartlets back into the oven on to the hot baking tray to cook until golden and set, about 30 minutes. Serve warm with several spoonfuls of the warm tomato and basil sauce and a crisp bitter leaf salad.

NOTE   Outside the big supermarkets ready ground hazelnuts are not very widely available, nor indeed are ready skinned ones; if you need to skin them, you first have to roast them. Spread the nuts in a single layer on a baking tray and bake at 180C/350F/Gas 4 for about 10 minutes. Cool slightly, then wrap the warm nuts in a tea towel and rub the nuts vigorously in the cloth to loosen as much of the skins as possible. When grinding nuts it is important not to overwork them as if you do so you will bring out their natural oils and will either end up with something resembling peanut butter or a greasy powder (which in this case would result in an unworkable pastry). The easiest solution here is to put cooled nuts in a food processor with all the flour for the pastry which will stop the oil separating from the nuts.

FOUR SERVINGS

THAI CHICKEN WITH BASIL

This is the very best of quick cooking. It is simplicity itself to prepare and cook and full of fresh and fragrant flavours. From Julie Sahni's *Savoring Spices and Herbs*.

4 chicken breasts, skinned and boned
8fl oz/1 cup/240ml chicken stock
8fl oz/1 cup/240ml coconut milk, tinned
1 fresh red chilli, seeded and finely chopped
1 star anise
1 tsp ground coriander
salt
3oz/6tbsp/90g skinned unsalted peanuts
1 tbsp sesame oil
2 garlic cloves, peeled and finely chopped
2 handfuls of basil leaves

Cut the chicken breasts across on a sharp diagonal into 1 inch/ 2.5cm strips. Put the stock, coconut milk and spices into a pan, bring to the boil and simmer gently for 10 minutes, when the sauce should have reduced by half.

Toast the peanuts in a dry pan over a slow heat until nutty and golden. Stir the chicken strips into the sauce and cook very gently until white, tender and cooked through. Take off the heat and adjust the seasoning.

Heat the oil and fry the garlic. When it starts to colour and crisp, throw in the basil and stir-fry briefly until just wilted. Stir the garlic-basil into the coconut chicken and serve at once with saffron rice, garnished with the toasted peanuts.

FOUR SERVINGS

CELERIAC GRATIN WITH TOMATO-CREAM SAUCE

This recipe comes from Patricia Wells' *At Home in Provence,* where it is called "celeriac lasagne", but Celia prefers this more elegant title. Choose a shallow dish with sloping low sides so that the celeriac develops a generous expanse of appetising crust (infact the French word *gratin* translates as "upper crust" and, like the English phrase, is used in a society as well as a culinary context).

Celeriac is often unfairly overlooked, which is a shame, because it's a jolly useful winter root which makes superb soups (on its own, or in partnership with blue cheese, with fennel or with wild mushrooms), marvellous mash (look back to *One Year At Books for Cooks No. 2*), and great gratins (as can be seen here, but try it also in a white winter root gratin with potatoes, parsnips, turnips, onions cooked with garlic and thyme either in cream or bechamel sauce). It also makes that most seasonal of winter salads, *celeriac rémoulade.*

for the sauce
2 tbsp olive oil
1 onion, peeled and finely chopped
3 garlic cloves, peeled and finely chopped
salt and pepper
28oz/800g tin of chopped Italian plum tomatoes

for the gratin
about 3lb/1½kg celeriac/celery root
6fl oz/¾ cup/180ml double/heavy cream
6oz/180g Parmesan, grated

Make the sauce. Warm the oil and soften the onion and garlic with a good pinch of salt, about 5 minutes. Add the tomatoes and simmer steadily for 15 minutes.

Peel the celeriac, cut into quarters and slice finely. Stir the celeriac slices into the tomato sauce — do this fairly speedily because celeriac turns brown if it hangs around too long. Gently simmer the celeriac in the sauce for about 10 minutes, until tender but still firm. Stir in the cream and adjust the seasoning.

Spread about half of the celeriac-tomato-cream into a buttered gratin dish, sprinkle over half of the grated cheese, spread over the rest of the celeriac and sprinkle with the rest of the cheese. Put into the oven and cook until nicely browned and tempting, about 40 minutes. Serve hot, with watercress and chicory (Belgian endive) salad with a hazelnut oil vinaigrette.

NOTE   The celeriac, sauce and cheese can be layered in the gratin dish several hours before cooking.

FOUR SERVINGS

45

Jennifer's Chicken Thighs Stewed in Balsamic Vinegar with Porcini Mushrooms & Sun-Dried Cherries served with Roasted Garlic Potato Puree

This is Jennifer's signature dish, cooked to great acclaim at one of our Books for Cooks special Christmas dinners. A supremely succulent stew served with the very monarch of mashed potatoes.

for the purée
a head of garlic
olive oil, salt and pepper
2lb/1kg floury/high starch potatoes, peeled
4oz/8tbsp/120g butter
4fl oz/½ cup/120ml olive oil
4fl oz/½ cup/120ml double/heavy cream

for the chicken
6 chicken thighs, skinned and boned
1oz/1½ cups/30g dried porcini
2 tbsp plain/all-purpose flour for coating
4oz/120g pancetta or streaky bacon in a piece, diced
1 onion, peeled and chopped
3 garlic cloves, peeled and chopped
4 tbsp dried cherries
8fl oz/1 cup/240ml red wine
4fl oz/½ cup/120ml chicken stock
4 tbsp balsamic vinegar
14oz/400g tin of peeled chopped Italian plum tomatoes
1 tsp arrowroot or cornstarch dissolved in 2 tsp cold water
a handful of flat-leaf parsley, chopped

Begin by roasting the garlic. Heat the oven to 180C/350F/Gas 4. Slice off the top quarter of the garlic bulb to expose the cloves. Put the garlic on a piece of foil, sprinkle with the olive oil, salt and pepper, wrap up and bake for 45 minutes. Take out of the oven and cool slightly before squeezing out the garlic pulp from the papery skins.

To make the stew, begin by soaking the dried porcini in hand-hot water for about half an hour. Lift them out, squeeze as much water as possible out of them and chop finely. Strain the soaking liquid through kitchen paper.

While the porcini are soaking, flour the chicken by putting the flour and a pinch each salt and pepper into a plastic bag with the chicken pieces and giving the bag a good shake while holding it tightly closed. Now fry the pancetta dice until they crispen and release all their fat. Scoop the pancetta out of the pan and put the floured chicken pieces in their fat. Fry until lightly golden on all sides, then lift out of the pan. Now put the onion and garlic into the pan to fry. When they are soft and yellow, stir in the dried cherries and porcini, pour in all the liquid, bring to the boil and simmer steadily for about 5 minutes. Now add the tomatoes, chicken and pancetta, turn the heat down to a mere flicker and cook gently for 40 minutes when the chicken will be very tender and the flavours fully developed. Correct the seasoning — you may want to add a quick splash of balsamic vinegar. Lastly stir in the arrowroot mixed with water to thicken the sauce to a nice coating consistency. Keep warm.

Make the purée while the chicken is cooking. Put the potatoes in a large pan of cold salted water. Bring to the boil and simmer, covered, until cooked. Drain them, and then put them back in the pan over a low heat to steam out any wateriness. Using either an electric beater or sheer muscle power, mash the potatoes to a smooth purée and then beat the butter, oil, cream, garlic and generous seasoning until the purée is really light and fluffy. Serve the stew on warmed plates sprinkled with parsley and accompanied by the roasted garlic potato purée.

NOTE Purées can be prepared several hours in advance and reheated either in a covered pan on a low heat or covered in a 150C/300F/Gas 2 oven.

FOUR SERVINGS

CALCUTTA FISH CAKES

Flecked green with herbs and coloured yellow with curry spices, these spicy fish cakes from Claudia Roden's *The Book of Jewish Food* make excellent finger food when scaled down to bite-sized proportions. We suggest a hot mango chutney to serve; if you shun store-bought products and are interested in preserving, look no further than Oded Schwartz's *Preserving* (London: Dorling Kindersley) — as well as an excellent hot mango chutney you'll find recipes for a stunning ginger chutney, a tremendous pumpkin chutney and much much more besides.

1lb/500g raw skinned white fish fillet
½ fresh green chilli, seeded
8 spring onions/scallions
a handful of parsley
¾ inch/2cm piece of fresh root ginger, peeled and chopped
1 tsp curry powder
1 tsp turmeric
a pinch of cayenne pepper
3 tbsp flour
½ tsp salt
sunflower oil for frying
parsley, mint or coriander/cilantro sprigs to decorate
best hot mango chutney to accompany

Put all the ingredients for the cakes except the fish in a food processor and work until finely chopped and well mixed. Add the fish fillet and, using the pulse button, work to a paste with the herbs — do not overprocess or you will end up with a creamy purée rather than a workable paste. Take lumps the size of a plum, roll into a ball and flatten slightly. You should have 16 little cakes in all. Heat a little oil in a frying pan over a moderate heat and cook the cakes in batches, turning over once, until crisp and golden brown. Drain them on kitchen paper. Serve with a mixture of steamed basmati and wild rice and the chutney: mound the rice in the middle of the plate and arrange the cakes and spoonfuls of the chutney alternately around the rice. Garnish with herb sprigs.

NOTE   It's actually a good idea to prepare the fish cakes several hours in advance; keep them covered and chilled.

FOUR SERVINGS

CHERMOULA MARINATED CHICKEN
WITH SPICY TOMATO-HONEY SAUCE
& BUTTERED COUSCOUS

In his *Dean & Deluca Cookbook*, David Rosengarten gives the classic Moroccan aromatic herb and spice rub chermoula an extra depth of flavour with the addition of chopped preserved lemon and black olives. The accompanying spicy sauce comes from Anna Thomas' *From Anna's Kitchen*. It was Jennifer who united these two good recipes in a great ensemble.

8 chicken thighs, skinned, boned and cut in half
parsley or coriander/cilantro sprigs to garnish

for the chermoula
a handful of flat-leaf parsley
a handful of coriander/cilantro
1 onion, peeled
3 garlic cloves, peeled
4 tbsp olive oil
1 tsp paprika
½ tsp ground cumin
½ tsp ground coriander
½ tsp ground ginger
8 black olives, stoned
1 preserved lemon (see page 51)
salt, pepper and cayenne pepper

for the sauce
2 tbsp olive oil
1 onion, peeled and finely chopped
6 garlic cloves, peeled and finely chopped
1 tsp ground cumin
1 tsp ground coriander
½ tsp ground cinnamon

1 tsp ground turmeric
½ tsp paprika
1lb/500g ripe fresh tomatoes, or 14oz/400g tin of
chopped Italian plum tomatoes and 2 tsp tomato purée
1 tbsp runny honey
salt, pepper and cayenne pepper
1 tbsp lemon juice

for the couscous
12oz/1½ cups/360g couscous
12fl oz/1½ cups/360 ml boiling chicken stock
2oz/4 tbsp/60g butter

Put all the chermoula ingredients except the olives and lemon in a food processor and work until finely chopped. Add the olives and lemon and, using the pulse button chop them coarsely into the herb and spice mixture. Smother the chicken pieces in the chermoula, cover with cling film (plastic wrap) and leave to marinate in the fridge for at least 2 hours or, better still, overnight.

Make the sauce by frying the onion and garlic in the oil until soft and yellow. Add the spices and stir-fry until toasted and fragrant, about 3 minutes. Stir in the tomatoes and gently simmer the sauce for 15-20 minutes until thickened. Correct the seasoning with the honey, salt, pepper, cayenne and lemon. Keep warm.

While the sauce is simmering, cook the chicken. Heat the oven to 200C/400F/Gas 6. Put the chicken pieces in a roasting dish and bake for 25 minutes until cooked through.

Prepare the couscous while the chicken is cooking. Put the grain in a large bowl, pour over the boiling stock and let it soak and swell for 15 minutes, then break up any lumps with a fork. Melt the butter, stir in the couscous and warm through over a gentle heat.

To serve, pile the couscous high in the middle of each warmed plate. Spoon over the spicy sauce and top with the chicken pieces. Garnish with herbs sprigs and serve at once.

FOUR SERVINGS

PRESERVED LEMONS

Preserved lemons are an essential ingredient in several of the recipes in this book and in many North African dishes. If preserving conjures not wholly agreeable images in your mind's eye (waving wooden spoons, looking for wrinkly skins on chilled saucers, obstinately runny jams, irritatingly solid chutneys), do not fear, this is real easy preserving. From Claudia Roden's *The Book of Jewish Food.*

Once made they become an invaluable condiment in the kitchen, contributing a supremely intense flavour, especially in partnership with turmeric and coriander (cilantro) in fish and chicken dishes. Refer to Claudia Roden's book for hugely inspiring recipes, or turn back to *One Year at Books for Cooks No. 1* and try the Moroccan Chicken with Lemons and Olives with the real thing.

5 lemons (choose them with thin skins)
about 5 tbsp salt
juice of about 3 lemons or more
1-2 tbsp olive oil

Wash and scrub the lemons. Quarter each lemon from the top to within ½ inch (1¼cm) of the stem end so that the sections are still attached. Carefully open out each lemon and sprinkle each one with about a teaspoon of salt, then close up and reshape the fruit. Put a tablespoon of salt in the bottom of a sterilised 16fl oz/2 cup/ 500ml jar with a rubber seal or an acid-proof lid and pack in the lemons, pushing them down well so that they are squashed together and sprinkling a little more salt in between the layers. Leave the jar to stand in a warm place (a sunny windowsill is ideal) for 3-4 days, when the juices will have been drawn out of the lemons. Press the lemons down again as much as you can, then pour in enough lemon juice to completely cover them. Before sealing the jar, pour a thin layer of olive oil on top of the juice to act as a protective film. Close the jar and leave to macerate and ripen for a month in a cool-ish place, when the lemons will be ready to eat.

Don't worry if the lemon juices turn a bit cloudy at first as they will clear naturally. There is no need to refrigerate them after opening.

To use preserved lemons, rinse them well under cold running water. Both the pulp and the peel can be used, although in most dishes the peel alone is called for; the lemon juices can be used again to preserve a new batch of lemons or try a splash in vinaigrettes, marindes and aromatic spiced stews.

KEEPS FOR 2 YEARS

NOTE To sterilise jars: put the jars on a kitchen paper-lined baking tray and put in a 160C/325F/Gas 3 for 10 minutes. Cool slightly before filling with a hot preserve; cool totally before filling with a cold preserve.

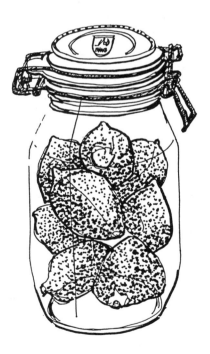

URSULA'S POLPETTE DI MELANZANE

Ursula is very grateful to the Amoroso family who taught her this recipe. They are Neapolitan aubergine producers and real experts on aubergine cooking and growing. The Italian word *polpette* translates as meat ball, but, Ursula tells us, aubergines are called poor man's meat throughout Southern Italy.

2 aubergines/eggplants, cut into small dice
salt and pepper
3 tbsp olive oil
3 free-range eggs, beaten
2½oz/75g Parmesan, grated
1oz/30g Pecorino, grated
7oz/200g mozzarella, cut into tiny dice
14oz/400g dry breadcrumbs
3½oz/100g pine nuts, finely chopped
a handful of flat-leaf parsley, finely chopped
1 rosemary sprig, leaves stripped and finely chopped
1 garlic clove, peeled and finely chopped

Begin by degorging the aubergines. Put them in a colander and sprinkle with 2 tsp salt. Mix the salt and aubergine dice together with your hands and leave to degorge for half an hour. Then put them in a clean tea towel and gently squeeze them dry. Warm the olive oil in your largest frying pan and, when it is hot, add the aubergine dice and stir-fry briskly until golden — you may have to do this in batches if you do not possess the requisite size pan.

Heat the oven to 200C/400F/Gas 6. Put the rest of the ingredients with the fried aubergine dice in a bowl and mix until well-combined. Form the aubergine mixture in *polpette* about the size and shape of a damson plum. Arrange them on an oiled baking tray and cook until hot and golden. Serve at once, either in solitary splendour on a bed of rocket (arugula), or in tandem with your very best tomato-basil sauce and lots of Parmesan shavings.

FOUR SERVINGS

CHICKEN WITH WALNUT AILLADE

Aillade is found all over the South West of France; it is a member of that family of intensely savoury nut pastes which includes Provençal pistou and Genoese pesto. Like its Mediterranean relatives, it is a veritable garlic lovers' dream. From Jennifer Paterson and Clarissa Dickson Wright's *Two Fat Ladies*.

8 chicken thighs, skinned and boned
5fl oz/⅔ cup/150ml thick creamy yoghurt
juice of 1 lemon
2½oz/75g walnut pieces
6 garlic cloves, peeled
2 handfuls (or a Portobello bunch) of flat-leaf parsley
juice of 1 lemon
3fl oz/6 tbsp/90ml walnut oil
2fl oz/4 tbsp/60ml sunflower oil
salt and pepper

Mix the yoghurt and lemon juice together, pour over the chicken and leave to marinate for half an hour.

Heat the oven to 190C/375F/Gas 5. Put the walnuts, garlic and parsley in a food processor and work until finely ground. Pour in the lemon juice, then slowly dribble in the oils. Correct the seasoning.

Put the yoghurt-coated chicken in a roasting dish and spread with the walnut-parsley paste. Bake for 45 minutes until the chicken is cooked. Serve hot with *haricots verts* tossed in good olive oil with chopped parsley and shallots.

FOUR SERVINGS

SWEET SOY GLAZED SALMON WITH CHERRY TOMATO-CUCUMBER RELISH & SOBA NOODLES

This recipe requires quite a few Japanese ingredients, but they are well worth having in your larder so you can make Japanese-style noodle soups and salads and flavour-boosted stir-fries, not to mention large quantities of this splendid glaze which keeps indefinitely in the fridge and does wonders for meat, poultry and oily fish. Rice vinegar is as its name implies made from rice and is much sweeter and milder than its occidental cousins. Mirin is a sweet, golden coloured wine also made from rice which is used only in cooking. Sake, the famous Japanese rice wine which should need no introduction, is used as much as for cooking as for drinking. Soba noodles are made from buckwheat and have that characteristic greyish brown buckwheat colour. As they are gluten-free, they are often available in healthfood shops. The glazed salmon came from Annie Bell's *More Taste Than Time,* the relish and noodles from Victoria and we think it's just perfection incarnate.

for the salmon
4 salmon fillets, with skin
2 tbsp sake
2 tbsp mirin
4 tbsp light soy sauce
1 tbsp sugar
½oz/15g butter
1 tbsp olive oil
1 tbsp pickled ginger, cut into matchsticks
1 lemon, cut into wedges

for the relish
8oz/250g cherry tomatoes, quartered
¼ cucumber, seeded and cut into small dice

3 spring onions/scallions, finely chopped
a handful of coriander/cilantro, finely chopped
1 tbsp rice vinegar
1 tbsp sunflower oil
salt and a pinch of cayenne pepper

for the noodles
8oz/250g soba noodles
1 tbsp each light and dark soy sauce
juice of 1 lime

Make the glaze by simmering the sake, mirin, soy sauce and sugar over a low heat for about 15 minutes until slightly thicker. Chill the glaze until thick and syrupy, about 2 hours.

To make the relish, combine all the ingredients and correct the seasoning. Cook the noodles according to the instructions on the packet, toss through with the soy sauces and lime juice and keep warm. Now cook the salmon. Have your grill very hot. Melt the butter with the oil in a pan and when it is hot slide in the salmon fillets, skin side down, and cook until crispy, about 5 minutes. Turn them over and colour very briefly on the other side, about 30 seconds. Take them out of the pan and drain well of fat on kitchen paper before painting the flesh side with most of the glaze and putting under the grill for about 2 minutes. Brush the salmon with the rest of the glaze and serve at once on warmed plates, with the relish spooned over and topped with the pickled ginger. Heap the noodles to one side of the plate and serve with the lemon wedges for squeezing.

FOUR SERVINGS

JENNIFER'S WARM ROASTED TOMATO BRUSCHETTA WITH RED ONION & BASIL VINAIGRETTE

The authentic *bruschetta al pommodoro* of sun-ripened tomatoes crushed on country bread toasted over wood embers is sadly out of the day to day reach of most of us. But help is definitely at hand with Jennifer's new twist on that time-honoured classic. Do have a go at using ripe tomatoes, though; Jennifer suggests leaving them on the window sill to ripen for a few days, and, if they remain obstinately pale and watery, dribbling over a little runny honey before roasting.

for the tomatoes
16 ripe plum tomatoes
2 garlic cloves, peeled and chopped
any fresh or dried herbs — herbes de Provence, fresh or dried thyme, fresh or dried rosemary
salt and pepper
4 tbsp olive oil
1 tbsp balsamic vinegar

for the vinaigrette
1 tbsp each red wine vinegar, sherry vinegar and raspberry vinegar
½ tsp Dijon mustard
1 garlic clove, peeled and crushed
1 red onion, peeled, halved and finely sliced
1 tbsp chopped fresh basil
6 tbsp best olive oil

4 large slices of ciabatta, cut ½ inch/1cm thick
4 handfuls of rocket/arugula

Begin by roasting the tomatoes. Heat the oven to 130C/250F/Gas 1.

Put the tomatoes in an oiled roasting dish. Scatter evenly with the garlic, herbs and seasoning and trickle over oil and vinegar. Put into the oven and roast for 2 hours.

When you have put the tomatoes in to roast, make the vinaigrette. Put all the ingredients in a jam jar, screw on the lid and shake vigorously until thick and creamy. Leave it to macerate until the tomatoes are ready or about an hour, when the flavours will have mingled and mellowed and the onions will be magenta pink.

Grill the bread to a golden brown on both sides and sprinkle with olive oil. Divide the rocket leaves between four plates, arranging them down one side of each plate. Put the grilled bread on the other side and divide the roasted tomatoes among each bread slice. Spoon the vinaigrette over the tomatoes and the rocket and serve while still warm.

FOUR SERVINGS

WINE-BRAISED GUINEA FOWL
WITH PRUNES & ALMONDS

Or, *faraona alla medici,* so called because it was apparently a favourite dish of that notorious dynasty of Florentine potentates, the Medici — indeed its medieval combination of meat with fruit and nuts conjures renaissance banquets and feasting. When Vivienne Gonley, author of *A Flavour of Tuscany,* recently began cooking in the Books for Cooks test kitchen, she treated us to this succulent dish.

2 guinea fowl, cut in eight portions each
2 tbsp olive oil
a rosemary sprig
a few sage leaves
2 onions, peeled and finely chopped
1 celery stick, finely chopped
2 carrots, peeled and diced
1 tbsp flour
half a bottle of red wine
6oz/180g stoned prunes
2oz/½ cup/60g pine nuts
4oz/1 cup/120g whole almonds, blanched and skinned
salt and pepper

Heat the oven to 200C/400F/Gas 6. In a heavy pan (with a lid), heat the oil and fry the guinea fowl pieces a few at a time until well-browned all over, taking them out of the pan as they brown. Pour out all but a tablespoon of fat from the pan. Put the meat back, sprinkle it with flour, throw in the onions, celery and carrots and put into the oven, uncovered, for 20 minutes.

Take the pan out of the oven pour in the wine, add the herbs, prunes and nuts, put back into the oven with the lid on for another 20 minutes.

Fish out the herbs and check the juices; if they are too liquid, take out the meat and put the pan over a high heat to bubble down until slightly thickened. Correct the seasoning of the sauce before putting the meat back into the pan. Serve with Jennifer's roasted garlic potato purée (see page 46).

NOTE   This dish can certainly be prepared the day before. Reheat in a hot oven.

FOUR SERVINGS

PAILLARD OF CHICKEN BREAST WITH PRESERVED LEMON COUSCOUS & PISTACHIO BUTTER

An innovative recipe from Andrew Blake in *Blakes* which marries North African ingredients with French techniques (*paillard,* so Eric tells us, is a culinary term dating from the mid nineteenth century) to great gastronomic effect

2oz/60g shelled, unsalted pistachio nuts
½ red chilli, seeded
5oz/150g butter, softened
3 tbsp chopped parsley
2 tbsp pomegranate syrup/molasses
2 tbsp orange juice
1 onion, peeled and finely chopped
2 garlic cloves, peeled and finely chopped
1 tbsp olive oil
12fl oz/1½ cups/360ml boiling chicken stock
12oz/1½ cups/360g couscous
½ preserved lemon, peel only, finely diced (see page 52)
salt and pepper
4 chicken breasts, skinned and boned
watercress or rocket/arugula leaves to garnish

Toast the nuts and chilli in a dry frying pan over a low heat until lightly browned. Chop finely, either by hand or in a food processor with pulse switch. Beat the butter until light and creamy, then stir in the nuts, chilli and parsley. Put the flavoured butter on to a rectangle of cling film, roll up into an even cylinder and chill until firm. Make a dressing by whisking the pomegranate syrup and orange juice together. Put the chicken breasts in between two sheets of cling film and lightly beat with rolling pin to an even thickness of ¼ inch (½ cm).

Warm the oil and gently fry the onion and garlic until softened but not coloured, about 5 minutes. Add the chicken stock, bring to the boil, pour over the couscous and, giving it a good stir, leave until it has absorbed all the stock and is swollen and tender, about 15 minutes, then break up any lumps with your fingers. Stir in the chopped preserved lemon, correct the seasoning and keep warm.

Heat a grill-pan until hot, brush the flattened chicken breast with oil and flash-grill for 3 minutes on each side. Be brave: the hotter the grill-pan, the less likely the chicken is to stick. Keep warm while you grill the rest of the chicken.

Divide the couscous between 4 warmed plates, heaping it up nicely in the middle of each plate. Put the grilled chicken on top and spoon the pomegranate-orange dressing around the plate. Slice the butter into four rounds, peel off the cling film and put on top of the chicken. Garnish with the greens and serve at once.

FOUR SERVINGS

63

ONION & THYME TART
WITH LEMON & HERB DRESSED BROCCOLI

A specially luxurious tart with a rich and quivering custard set in a puff pastry shell from Annie Bell's *More Taste Than Time*. (Try other flavourings: we found smoked salmon slices and chopped leek stewed in butter a particularly appetising combination.) Victoria found that the lemony broccoli makes a light and fresh accompaniment to this opulent tart.

for the tart
8oz/250g puff pastry
2lb/1kg onions, peeled, quartered and finely sliced
1oz/2tbsp/30g butter
salt
8fl oz/1 cup/240ml double/heavy cream
6fl oz/¾ cup/180ml milk
1 free-range egg and 2 yolks, beaten
1 tbsp freshly grated Parmesan
6 sprigs of thyme, leaves stripped
pepper and grated nutmeg

for the broccoli
1 onion, peeled and finely chopped
6 garlic cloves, peeled and finely chopped
2 thyme sprigs, leaves stripped
2 tbsp finely chopped parsley
grated zest and juice of 2 lemons
4fl oz/½ cup/120ml olive oil
1lb/500g broccoli, divided into large florets

First make the dressing for the broccoli. Put all the ingredients except the broccoli into a jar, put on the lid, shake vigorously and leave to macerate.

Put a baking tray into the oven and heat to 190C/375F/Gas 5.

Roll out the pastry and line a 9½ inch/24cm springform cake tin (that is, a cake tin with a removable base) with the pastry lifted into place on the rolling pin. Trim the edges by rolling the pin over the top of the tin, pressing down to cut off the extra pastry and prick the bottom of the pastry case with a fork. Now line the pastry case with baking parchment, fill with baking beans, put into the oven on to the hot baking tray and cook for 15 minutes. Take out the paper and the beans and bake for another 15 minutes when the pastry should be lightly golden and the bottom dried out and cooked.

Cook the onions while the pastry case is baking. Melt the butter, stir in the onions and a good pinch of salt and stew slowly, with the lid on, stirring often, for 40 minutes, until the onions are meltingly soft and not at all browned.

When the onions are cooked and the pastry baked, beat together the rest of the ingredients and season with pepper and nutmeg. Spread the onions evenly over the pastry case and put over the egg-cream mixture. Put into the oven on to the hot baking tray (which will hopefully mean no soggy pastry) and cook for 30-40 minutes until golden and set.

While the tart is cooling slightly, steam or simmer the broccoli until tender, dress with the lemon dressing and serve at once with the warm tart.

FOUR SERVINGS

VICTORIA'S SALAD OF SMOKED FISH
ROASTED CHERRY TOMATOES & ROCKET
WITH CHERVIL-DILL VINAIGRETTE

Faced with the challenge of catering for a party of delightful but exacting French *gourmands*, Victoria was determined to show English cooking at its best. This is what she served as a starter, but it makes a lovely luncheon dish too. Once assembled it looks terribly pretty and summery with its pinks and greens highlighted by the red tomatoes.

for the salad
12oz/350g smoked trout slices
8 cooked jumbo prawns/shrimp, shelled
8 cherry tomatoes, cut in half
salt and pepper
1 tsp balsamic vinegar
1 tbsp olive oil
3 handfuls of rocket/arugula
2 tbsp tiny capers, washed and drained
chervil sprigs to garnish

for the vinaigrette
2 tbsp chopped fresh dill
2 tbsp chopped fresh chervil
1 tsp Dijon mustard
a pinch of sugar
2 tbsp red wine vinegar
2 tbsp sunflower oil
3 tbsp olive oil
salt and pepper

Heat the oven to 180C/350F/Gas 4. Put the cherry tomatoes in a roasting dish and sprinkle with the seasoning, oil and vinegar and roast for 20 minutes until lightly wilted. Cool to room temperature.

Make the dressing by putting all the ingredients in a jam jar, srewing on the lid and shaking vigorously until thick and emulsified.

To assemble the salad, put a twirl of smoked fish in the middle of each plate and arrange 2 prawns per person to one side. Top the fish with the rocket leaves, then scatter the whole plate with capers and dot with cherry tomato halves. Spoon over the vinaigrette just before serving and decorate with sprigs of chervil.

FOUR SERVINGS

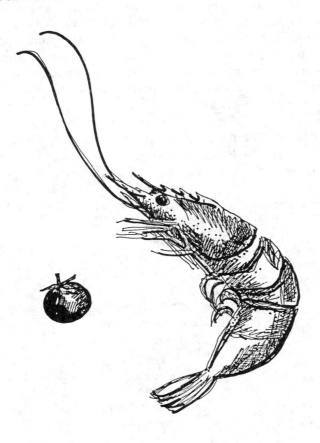

MIDDLE EASTERN MEAT BALLS WITH SMOKY AUBERGINE PURÉE & MINTED YOGHURT

These meat balls from Stephanie Alexander's *The Cook's Companion* are eminently versatile. Knead 4 tablespoons of toasted pine nuts into the meat ball mixture for an interestingly textured variation. Roll them in to smaller marble-sized balls to make lovely party finger foods with the smoky purée as a dip; or serve them as part of a buffet table at room temperature with a couscous salad stirred through with lots of chopped herbs and diced tomato dressed with olive oil and lemon. If you object to frying, gently simmer them in middle eastern style tomato sauce spiced with cumin, cinnamon and cayenne and garnished with plenty of chopped parsley.

As for the purée, cooking an aubergine directly over a flame is certainly messier than grilling or roasting but it imparts that distinctive smoky flavour which you just can't get unless you barbecue them. The purée makes an easy canapé spooned on to crostini and garnished with toasted sesame seeds and mint sprigs, or a simple but good whole meal served chilled with plenty of hot bread and a ripe tomato salad, so really it is better to make more rather than less and keep it in the fridge as a useful standby.

for the purée
1 aubergine/eggplant
1 garlic clove, peeled
a large pinch of salt
juice of ½ lemon
1 tbsp thick creamy yoghurt
2 tbsp olive oil
cayenne pepper

for the yoghurt
4fl oz/½ cup/120ml thick creamy yoghurt
a handful of fresh mint, finely chopped

for the meat balls

1lb/500g lean lamb or beef or a combination, minced
1 onion, peeled and roughly chopped (if you have a food
processor) or grated (if you do not)
1 garlic clove, peeled and crushed
a handful of coriander/cilantro, chopped
2 tsp ground cumin
1 tsp ground allspice
2 tsp salt
a pinch of cayenne
olive oil for frying

Pierce the aubergine in a few places with the point of a knife and turn them directly over a flame (or under an overhead grill) until the skin is thoroughly (and we mean thoroughly) black and blistered and the flesh feels soft. Mash the garlic to a paste with a good pinch of salt and the flat blade of a knife. When the aubergine has cooled enough to handle, peel off the charred skin and squeeze out as much moisture as possible from the flesh. Work the aubergine to a purée, either in a blender or food processor or by chopping and then mashing with a potato masher. Beat in the rest of the ingredients a little at a time and keep tasting. Stir the chopped mint into the yoghurt before turning your attention to the meat balls.

Work all the meat ball ingredients until soft and paste-like, either with a minute or so of blasting in a food processor or 5 minutes of vigorous kneading by hand. With wet hands (to stop the mixture sticking), divide the mixture into 24 pieces and roll into walnut-sized balls. Heat the oil over a moderate heat until it sizzles and fry the meat balls, a few at a time, for about 5 minutes, turning them so that they are crisp and browned all over but still moist and juicy inside. Drain well on kitchen paper and keep warm until all the meat balls have been fried. Serve hot with a few spoonfuls each of the minted yoghurt and smoky aubergine purée and a simple green salad dressed with lemon juice and olive oil. Warm flat bread is a must.

FOUR SERVINGS

PUY LENTILS WITH DILL, SALSA VERDE, ROASTED PEPPERS & FETA CHEESE

We found this dish in Rena Salaman's *Healthy Mediterranean Cooking* — and its combination of white cheese, red peppers, green dressing makes it as colourful as it is healthful. This is an excellent version of the classic Italian sauce salsa verde and we urge you to make good use of it, especially with grilled foods.

12oz/1½ cups/360g Puy lentils
4 red peppers, quartered, stemmed and seeded
a handful of dill, roughly chopped
salt and pepper
2 handfuls of baby salad leaves
1 tbsp olive oil
1 tsp vinegar
8oz/250g Feta cheese, diced
dill sprigs to decorate

for the salsa
2 fresh green chillies, seeded and finely chopped
3 garlic cloves, peeled and finely chopped
½ inch/1½cm piece of root ginger, peeled and finely chopped
a handful of flat-leaf parsley
a handful of fresh dill
1 tsp Dijon mustard
juice of 1½ lemons
3 tbsp olive oil

Rinse the lentils, cover them generously with water, bring to the boil and simmer steadily until cooked, which will take anything from 20 to 40 minutes, depending on age, so you will have to keep testing to see if they are done.

While the lentils are cooking, put the pepper quarters skin side up under a hot grill and roast until charred and blistered all over.

Now put them in a bowl, cover with a tea towel, and leave for 10 minutes while the trapped steam loosens the pepper skins so they may easily be slipped off. Cut the peeled peppers into neat squares.

Make the salsa. Put all the ingredients in a food processor and work until smooth. Stir the salsa into the drained but still warm lentils with the red peppers. Cover and leave to marinate for a couple of hours.

Lightly dress the salad leaves with the oil and vinegar and divide them among 4 plates. Stir the chopped dill into the lentils and mound them up on the bed of salad leaves. Dot the salad evenly with the Feta dice and dill sprigs. Serve at once.

NOTE   Cooked, drained and cooled lentils keep very well covered and chilled for up to a week. But lentils served straight out of the fridge are really quite insipid, so do let them get back to room temperature before serving.

FOUR SERVINGS

DUCK BREASTS WITH SWEET TOMATO-SESAME CHUTNEY

This dish received universal approbation when Victoria tried it out in the test kitchen. We think it was the sweetly spiced chutney which won the day. From Annie Bell's *More Taste Than Time*.

for the chutney
1lb/500g ripe tomatoes
6fl oz/¾ cup/180ml white wine vinegar
6oz/¾ cup/180ml caster/granulated sugar
¼ tsp fennel seeds, crushed
pinch each cayenne pepper and ground ginger
¼ tsp curry powder
4 cardamom pods
1 bay leaf
½oz/1½ tbsp/15g raisins
1 tbsp sesame seeds
salt

4 duck breasts
salt and pepper
toasted sesame seeds and spring onion/scallion slivers to garnish

With a small knife cut the core end out of the tomatoes and put them in a bowl. Pour over boiling water to cover and leave for a minute, when the skins should peel off easily. Roughly chop the peeled tomatoes.

Heat the vinegar and the sugar over a low heat, stirring until the sugar has completely dissolved. Then stop stirring, raise the heat, bring to the boil and add the tomatoes and all the herbs and spices. Simmer steadily for about 20 minutes, then fish out the bay leaf and cardamom pods and add the raisins and sesame seeds. Cook gently for about 10 minutes, stirring to stop sticking.

Heat the oven to 190C/375F/Gas 5. Score the skin of the duck breasts in a cross-hatch pattern. Heat a heavy frying pan over a moderate flame, and, when it is hot, put in the duck breasts, skin side down, and cook for about 5 minutes, until the fat has melted and the skin browned. Pour off the fat, turn the breasts over and put into the oven to roast for 10 minutes, when they should still be pink, or 12 minutes for *à point*. Test them with the point of a knife to check. Take them out of the pan and let them rest (either wrapped in foil or on a dish in the turned off oven with the door slightly open) for 5 minutes. We like this dish best with plenty of buttered couscous (see page 49) and a green leaf salad dressed with a mint vinaigrette. Heap up the couscous nicely on one side of 4 warmed plates and arrange the salad on the other side. Then slice each duck breast across on the diagonal and fan out on top of the couscous, crispy skin side up. Top with a generous spoonful of the sweetly spiced chutney and sprinkle with toasted sesame seeds and slivers of spring onion. Serve at once.

FOUR SERVINGS

GOAT'S CHEESE, FENNEL & OLIVE TART
WITH RED PEPPER SAUCE

A recipe from *Blakes* by Andrew Blake which unites colour and flavour with equal intensity. The white cheese and black olives set in a thyme-scented yellow custard served with a splash of red smoky sauce make for a very pretty plate. Victoria pairs this savoury tart with halved new potatoes, oven roasted until crisp, and tossed with young spinach leaves and a balsamic shallot vinaigrette.

2 red peppers, quartered and cored
1 fennel bulb, quartered and finely sliced
1½oz/3 tbsp/45g butter
5oz/150g goat's cheese log, diced
1½oz/45g kalamata olives, stoned and halved
3 sprigs of thyme, leaves stripped
3 free-range eggs, beaten
8fl oz/1 cup/240ml double/heavy cream
salt and pepper
9½/24cm shortcrust pastry case, baked blind/pre-baked
(see pages 122-4)

If you do not possess an over-head grill independent from your oven, you had better make the sauce first; if, however, you are lucky enough to have a separate grill, save time by making it while the tart bakes. Put the pepper quarters skin side up under a hot grill and cook until charred and blistered all over. Now put them in a bowl, cover with a tea towel, and leave for 10 minutes while the trapped steam loosens the pepper skins so they may easily be slipped off. Put the peeled pepper quarters into a blender and work to a purée; adjust the seasoning and consistency: you may want to add a little sugar, maybe a little Tabasco, to boost the flavour, as well as salt and pepper, and stir in a little water to thin it down slightly.

Put a baking tray in the oven and heat to 190C/375F/Gas 5. Melt the butter and slowly stew the fennel until softened, about 10 minutes. Arrange the fennel evenly in the pastry case, dot with the goat's cheese, scatter with olives and sprinkle with thyme. Beat the eggs and cream together, season (remembering that you have olives and mature goat's cheese to take into consideration) and pour into the pastry case. Put into the oven on to the hot baking tray — this tactic should avoid soggy pastry — and cook for 30 minutes, or until golden and set.

Let the tart cool a little before cutting and serving each slice in a pool of the red pepper sauce.

FOUR SERVINGS

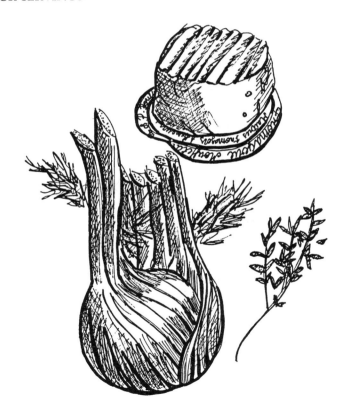

CELIA'S GRILLED AUBERGINE & POLENTA
STACKS WITH BEETROOT SALSA

A truly impressive summertime dish, big on colour and flavour. Once you've cooked and cooled your polenta (which can be done the day before), it's relatively quick and easy to assemble. Celia suggests selecting aubergines, onions and tomatoes which have roughly the same circumference.

for the stacks
3 pints/7 cups/1¾ litres water
8oz/1⅔ cups/240g coarse-grained polenta/Italian
yellow cornmeal
1 tbsp salt
2 large Spanish/sweet onions, peeled
2 aubergines/eggplants
2 ripe beefsteak tomatoes
olive oil and balsamic vinegar
salt and pepper
Parmesan shavings and rocket/arugula leaves to decorate

for the salsa
4 beetroot
juice of 2 lemons
a handful of coriander/cilantro, finely chopped
a handful of flat-leaf parsley, finely chopped
salt, pepper and a pinch of sugar

First make the polenta. Bring the water to the boil in a large, heavy pan. Add the salt, and, keeping the water at a steady simmer, gradually add the polenta, letting a fistful run through the fingers of one hand in a very thin stream, while the other hand stirs constantly to prevent lumps. When you have put in all the polenta, continue to stir vigorously while it bubbles gently for about 30-40 minutes. The polenta is cooked when it is very thick and soft and pulls away from the sides of the pan. Pour it on to a dampened baking tray and spread it flat to a thickness of ½ inch (1cm). Leave it for about an hour or until cold and set.

Make the salsa by boiling the beetroot in their skins until tender, about half an hour. Drain and rub off the skins under cold running water. Cut the cooked beetroot into even dice and mix together with the rest of the salsa ingredients.

Heat the oven to 200C/400F/Gas 6. Slice the onions into 8 rounds about ½ inch (1cm) thick. Put them on a baking tray, brush with oil and sprinkle with salt and pepper. Slice the aubergine into 8 rounds ¾ inch (2cm) thick. Brush them with oil, season them and put one piece of aubergine on top of each piece of onion. Roast until the aubergines are nicely coloured, about half an hour. Slice the tomatoes into 8 rounds ½ inch (1cm) thick. When the aubergine-onion stacks are cooked, top each one with a tomato slice and sprinkle with oil, vinegar and seasoning. Finely chop any bits of onion or tomato you have left over and add them to the salsa.

Now stamp the cooled polenta into rounds the same size as your vegetable rounds with a dampened glass or pastry cutter: you want 16, which you put on a lightly oiled baking tray. Brush them with oil.

To finish the cooking, you can either bake the polenta rounds and vegetable stacks in the hot oven for 15 minutes or, if pressed for time, put them under a hot grill for a few minutes until sizzling.

Assemble the stacks by arranging 2 polenta rounds on each plate. Top each round with a vegetable stack, then finish with another piece of polenta. Spoon the salsa over and around the polenta-vegetable stacks and decorate with the rocket leaves and Parmesan shavings. Serve at once.

NOTE Cooked and cooled polenta will keep covered tightly with cling film for several days in the refrigerator.

FOUR SERVINGS

Beef Daube with Mustard, Herbs & White Wine

This is real slow food *par excellence* from Patricia Wells' *At Home in Provence*. The winey, tarragon-scented steam fills the room, making you drunk on flavour, as you lift the lid off the pan after the daube's long cooking.

> 1½lb/750g *stewing beef, cut into 4 inch/10cm pieces*
> 1 *celery stick*, 2 *bay leaves and* 3 *sprigs each of parsley,*
> *thyme and tarragon*
> 3 *tbsp olive oil*
> *salt and pepper*
> 1 *bottle of dry white wine*
> 2 *tbsp Dijon mustard*
> 3 *onions, peeled, halved and finely sliced*
> 4 *garlic cloves, peeled and halved*
> 14oz/400g *chopped Italian plum tomatoes*
> *more chopped tarragon to finish*

Make a *bouquet garni* by cutting the celery stick in half, sandwiching the herbs in the middle and binding with kitchen string to make a neat bundle.

Warm the oil in a heavy pan (which must have a close-fitting lid) over a moderate flame. When it is hot, sear the beef pieces; put only a few at a time in the pan (too many and they will steam rather than fry) and brown them rapidly but thoroughly on all sides. Put the pieces aside when done, sprinkle with salt and pepper, and carry on till all the beef is browned and out of the pan.

Next pour in the wine and bring to the boil. Vigorously scrape up all crusty caramelised juices from the bottom of the pan and let the wine simmer steadily for about 5 minutes, when all the alcohol should have bubbled away. Stir in the mustard until evenly blended, then add the beef and all the rest of the ingredients. Cover the pan, first with a piece of foil and then with the lid and, turning the heat down to a flicker, let it barely simmer on top of the stove or in a 150C/300F/Gas 2 oven for 2 to 3 hours. Take care that the daube does not actually boil; boiling will simply toughen the meat.

When the daube is cooked and the meat meltingly tender, fish out the *bouquet garni*. If the daube looks too liquid, scoop out all the meat with a slotted spoon and boil down the winey juices until concentrated. Put the meat back and stir in the chopped tarragon. Serve at once, with a creamy potato gratin, a roasted garlic potato purée (see Jennifer's on page 46) or noodles tossed in butter, parsley and Parmesan.

FOUR SERVINGS

NOTE   Daubes, braises and stews are always better cooked the day before, and this one is no exception.

Fennel Gratin with Cream & Parmesan

You must have noticed by now that we have a bit of a fennel theme running through the book. It was aubergines in our first book, beetroot in our second and this year fennel steps into the spotlight. We love its clean crisp texture and cool anise-scented flavour. It is also an exceptionally versatile vegetable, raw or cooked: it steams, braises, sautés, bakes, roasts and grills with equal success. Since it is at its best over the winter months from autumn to spring, it makes a welcome addition (thinly sliced or finely chopped) to winter salads.

This simple and very good dish just had to go in. As well as featuring in Ursula's *Real Fast Vegetarian,* it is also a great favourite of Heidi Lascelles, founder and proprietor of Books for Cooks.

4 fennel bulbs
salt and pepper
2oz/60g Parmesan, grated
½ pint/1¼ cups/300ml double/heavy cream

Heat the oven to 200C/400F/Gas 6. Pull off the tough outer layers of the fennel bulbs and cut the fennel tops where they meet the bulbs (use these trimmings for stock-making and any feathery fronds for chopping and sprinkling). Slice about ⅛ inch (4mm) from the root end and cut the bulbs lengthwise into quarters. Drop the fennel quarters in plenty of salted simmering water and cook for about 7 minutes, when the root end of the quarters should feel tender but firm when prodded with a fork. Drain very well and arrange the fennel quarters in one layer in a well-buttered gratin dish. Sprinkle with salt, pepper and cheese, pour over the cream and put into the oven for about 20 minutes. The cream will bubble up around the fennel and the top will brown appetisingly. Serve hot with a simple green leaf salad dressed with lemon, olive oil and grated Parmesan and plenty of warm Italian bread.

NOTE Fennel versatility is very much in evidence in this little book alone: find it simmered and puréed in a delicate cream soup (page 8), stewed with saffron and chicken in a colourful and full-flavoured Provençal dish (page 22), sautéed and baked in a tart with goat's cheese and olives (page 74), darkly and deeply caramelised with onions (page 84) and holding its own in a vegetable triumvirate featuring also tomatoes and spinach for a very special lasagne (page 88).

FOUR SERVINGS

PISTACHIO-CRUSTED FISH
WITH SAFFRON MASHED POTATOES &
MASALA SAUCE

New dish, old theme from Andrew Blake in *Blakes*. Curry sauce was a favourite fish accompaniment, since fallen from favour, except in our on-going British passion for kedgeree. This is Grown Up Nursery Food and we love it.

About coconut cream: don't shake the tin of coconut milk as you usually do, but open it and leave it for a minute or two when you'll find that the heavier cream of coconut settles to the bottom and you can easily pour off the thinner coconut milk.

for the sauce
2 tbsp sunflower oil
1 tbsp sesame oil
1 onion, peeled and finely chopped
2 garlic cloves, peeled and finely chopped
1 inch/2½cm piece of fresh root ginger, peeled and finely chopped
2 fresh red chillies, seeded and finely chopped
1 tsp ground coriander
½ tsp ground cumin
1 tsp turmeric
¼ tsp ground cinnamon
2 tbsp tomato purée
4fl oz/½ cup/120ml coconut cream (see note above)
1 tbsp palm sugar or dark brown sugar
1 pint/2½ cups/600ml chicken or vegetable stock
1 tbsp fish sauce

for the potatoes
2lb/1kg potatoes, peeled
8fl oz/1 cup/240ml milk
1 tsp of saffron threads or saffron powder, infused in 2 tbsp hot water
1 garlic clove, peeled and chopped

4oz/1 stick/120g butter
salt and pepper

for the fish
5oz/1¼ cups/150g unsalted shelled pistachio nuts
2lb/1kg white fish fillet, cut into 4 portions
coriander/cilantro sprigs to garnish

Warm the oils in a wide pan and fry the onion, garlic, ginger and chillies until the onion just starts to catch round the edges. Add the spices and stir-fry until the onions are spicily fragrant. Add the tomato purée, coconut cream and sugar and cook until just beginning to bubble. Pour in the stock, bring to the boil and simmer steadily until well-reduced and the sauce coats the back of a spoon, about half an hour. Strain through a sieve to make a smooth sauce before adding the fish sauce and correcting the seasoning. Keep warm.

While the sauce is bubbling away, make the mashed potatoes. Heat together the milk, saffron in its water and garlic until just below boiling point. Cover, turn off the heat and leave to infuse while you cook the potatoes. Put the potatoes in a large pan of cold salted water. Bring to the boil and simmer, covered, until cooked. Drain them, and then put them back in the pan over a low heat to steam out any wateriness. Mash the potatoes very thoroughly and then beat the saffron-garlic milk, the butter and generous seasoning until the purée is really light and fluffy. Keep warm.

Heat the oven to 200C/400F/Gas 6. Roughly chop the pistachio nuts in a food processor. Season the fish fillets with salt and pepper before sprinking evenly with the chopped pistachios. Put the fish in a lightly oiled roasting dish, put into the oven and roast for 8-10 minutes or until cooked through.

To serve, spoon the saffron mashed potatoes into the middle of each plate, surround with the masala sauce, top with the pistachio-crusted cod and garnish with coriander sprigs. Serve at once.

FOUR SERVINGS

SALAD OF PEPPERY GREENS, PEARS, WALNUTS & ROQUEFORT WITH CARAMELISED FENNEL & ONION BRUSCHETTA

A sensational salad from Anna Thomas' *From Anna's Kitchen*. The caramelised fennel-onion-olive mixture also makes a good and unusual pasta sauce.

for the bruschetta
2 onions, peeled and finely sliced
2 fennel bulbs, trimmed, quartered and finely sliced
1 tbsp olive oil
½oz/1 tbsp/15g butter
2fl oz/4 tbsp/60ml white wine
8 black olives, stoned and sliced
salt and pepper
4 large slices of ciabatta, cut ½ inch/1cm thick
olive oil

for the salad
2 handfuls of rocket/arugula
1 head of chicory/Belgian endive, leaves separated
1 handful of watercress
1 pear
juice of ½ lemon
4 tbsp walnut pieces, toasted
4oz/120g Roquefort, crumbled
2 tbsp balsamic vinegar
4 tbsp olive oil
salt and pepper

Bégin with the bruschetta. Melt the butter with the oil in a non-stick or heavy-bottomed pan, stir in the sliced onion and fennel and stew slowly for about three-quarters of an hour until the vegetables are golden brown and tender, stirring from time to time. Add the wine and olives and continue cooking until the wine has bubbled away. Correct the seasoning and keep warm.

Grill the bread until golden brown on both sides and sprinkle with a little olive oil. Toast the walnut pieces in a dry pan over a slow heat until lightly coloured and nuttily aromatic. Peel, quarter, core and finely slice the pear and toss with the lemon juice to discourage any discolouration.

Put all the ingredients for the salad in a large bowl and mix gently until thoroughly dressed. Correct the seasoning before dividing the salad among 4 plates, heaping it up nicely. Put a slice of grilled bread on top of each salad and spoon over the hot caramelised fennel-onion mixture. Serve at once.

FOUR SERVINGS.

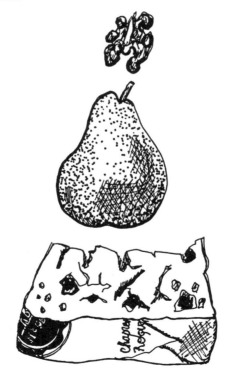

BARBADIAN SEASONED CHICKEN WITH AVOCADO SALSA & GINGERED SWEET POTATO MASH

From Annie Bell's *More Taste Than Time*. She recommends quite indiscriminate use of this delicious seasoning (properly called bajun and hailing from the Caribbean island of Barbados) and we agree; use it to marinate meat, fish and vegetables before grilling or, better still, barbecuing. Victoria devised the salsa and mash to complete the totally tropical taste.

4 free-range chicken breasts, boned and skinned
4 spring onions/scallions, finely chopped
½ red onion, skinned and finely chopped
1 fresh red chilli, seeded and finely chopped
a handful of parsley, finely chopped
8 thyme sprigs, leaves stripped
salt and pepper
juice of 1 lime
3 tbsp olive oil

for the mash
2lb/1kg orange sweet potatoes, peeled (butternut squash or good pumpkin makes a nice variation)
1oz/2 tbsp/30g butter
1 tbsp olive oil
2 garlic cloves, peeled and finely chopped
1 inch/2½cm fresh root ginger, peeled and chopped
juice of ½ lemon
salt, pepper and freshly grated nutmeg

for the salsa
1 avocado
juice of 1 lime
½ red onion, peeled and finely chopped

a handful of mint or coriander/cilantro, finely chopped
2 tbsp olive oil

Mix the finely chopped onions, chilli and herbs together and stir in the seasoning, lime juice and oil. With a sharp knife score the chicken breasts: make 3 cuts on the diagonal ¼ inch (5mm) deep on one side. Smother each chicken breast on both sides with the seasoning mixture, pushing well into the cuts. Wrap in cling film, put in refrigerator to chill and marinate for at least half an hour and up to 2 hours.

Cook the sweet potatoes in boiling salted water until tender, then drain and mash until smooth. Melt the butter with the oil and soften the garlic and ginger for about 5 minutes. Stir this into the mashed potatoes with the lemon juice and correct the seasoning.

Make the salsa just before cooking the chicken. Peel, halve, stone and dice the avocado. Mix the avocado dice with the rest of the salsa ingredients and correct the seasoning.

Cook the chicken under a hot grill about 6 inches (15cm) from the heat for about 10 minutes. Turn the chicken over and grill for another 8 minutes until nicely coloured. The juices should run clear when the meat is pierced with a sharp knife or skewer.

Divide the mash between 4 warmed plates, mounding it up nicely. Slice the chicken across on the diagonal and fan them out on the plates, slightly overlapping the mash. Pile the salsa on top of the chicken and serve with a wedge of lime.

FOUR SERVINGS

URSULA'S SPINACH, FENNEL & TOMATO LASAGNE

A multi-coloured, multi-flavoured lasagne devised by Ursula for a really celebratory vegetarian meal.

For sheer ease, we use pre-cooked lasagne, but have to admit that any lasagne is infinitely superior if you make your own pasta; bought is never as thin and silkin as home-made. Want to know how? Simply come to one of Ursula's pasta workshops!

for the sauce
1 pint/2½ cups/580ml milk
1 onion, peeled and quartered
1 bay leaf
6 peppercorns
1½oz/3 tbsp/45g butter
1¼oz/35g plain flour
salt, pepper and freshly grated nutmeg

about 9 sheets of pre-cooked lasagne
6 ripe plum tomatoes
2 garlic cloves, peeled and finely chopped
1 tbsp olive oil
6oz/180g mozzarella, sliced
1 fennel bulb
1lb/500g spinach
grated zest of 1 lemon
12oz/360g ricotta
4oz/120g Parmesan, grated
a handful of basil

Begin by infusing the milk. Put the milk with the onion, bay and peppercorns in a pan, bring just to the boil, turn off the heat, cover and leave to infuse while you prepare the other ingredients.

Heat the oven to 180C/350F/Gas 4. Cut the tomatoes in half

and arrange them cut side up on a baking tray. Sprinkle them with salt, pepper, garlic and oil and bake them until softened and wilted, about 35 minutes.

Pull off the tough outer layers of the fennel bulb and cut the fennel tops where they meet the bulbs. Slice about ⅛ inch (4mm) from the root end and cut lengthwise into thin slices. Drop the fennel into plenty of salted simmering water and cook for about 5 minutes, when the root end of the quarters should feel tender but firm when prodded with a fork. Drain very well.

Put the spinach in a pan with ½ inch/1cm water. Cover the pan and cook the spinach over a high heat until the leaves start to wilt. Stir, cover and cook until the spinach is completely wilted, which will take only a minute or two. Drain the spinach in a colander and, when cooled slightly, squeeze it dry with your hands. Form the spinach in small, marble-sized balls.

Beat the lemon zest with about half of the grated Parmesan into the ricotta and correct the seasoning.

Now finish the béchamel sauce. Melt the butter, stir in the flour and cook gently for about a minute, stirring all the time, until quite smooth and the palest yellow. Take the pan off the heat and pour in the milk through a sieve to strain out the vegetables, whisking very briskly until absolutely smooth. Put the pan back on the heat and bring back to the boil, whisking all the time until the sauce thickens. Correct the seasoning with salt, pepper and nutmeg and simmer gently for a minute or two. If you do end up with lumps in your sauce, do not despair, just push it through a sieve.

To assemble the lasagne you need a buttered baking dish about 9 by 9 inches (23 by 23cm) or thereabouts. Pour half the sauce into the bottom of the dish and cover with a single player of pasta. Spread the pasta with half of the ricotta mixture and arrange the tomato halves, sliced mozzarella, basil leaves and fennel slices (in that order) evenly on top. Follow this with another layer of pasta spread with the rest of the ricotta and dotted with the balls of spinach. Arrange a final layer of pasta on top, pour over the rest of the sauce and sprinkle evenly with the remaining grated Parmesan. Put the lasagne into the oven and cook until golden and bubbling, about half an hour. Serve at once, with a simple green leaf salad dressed with lemon and oil.

NOTE   Lasagne is well known as an easy prepare-ahead dinner party dish and it was this fact which probably contributed to the over popularisation and subsequent debasement of the traditional *lasagne al forno.* Ursula's lasagne in common with the meat lasagnes can be assembled the day before and kept covered and chilled until ready to bake.

One more thing, here in Europe, shop-bought lasagne tends to measure about 3¼ by 6½ inches (8 by 16½cm).

FOUR SERVINGS

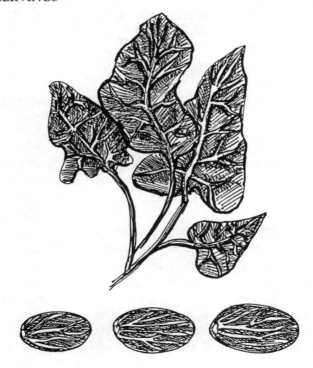

Cakes and Tarts

CHOCOLATE HAZELNUT TORTE

Victoria is always looking for new recipes to add to her chocolate repertoire, but, although many can be very good, not every recipe tested is a true great. This one, however, with its orange-scented overtones, moist nutty texture and luscious chocolate ganache glaze, made it well past the finishing post. It's good with fromage frais, excellent with crème fraîche, outstanding with vanilla ice-cream. From Emily Luchetti's *Four Star Desserts*.

for the cake
5oz/1¼ cups hazelnuts, roasted and skinned
(see note)
1oz/¼ cup/30g plain/cake flour
6oz/1½ sticks/180g butter
6oz/180g plain/bittersweet chocolate,
broken into pieces
4 free-range eggs, separated
6oz/1 cup/180g caster/granulated sugar
¼ tsp salt
grated zest of 1 orange

for the glaze
3fl oz/6 tbsp/90ml double/heavy cream
6oz/180g plain/bittersweet chocolate,
broken into pieces
1½ tbsp golden syrup/light corn syrup
1 tbsp brandy
½ tbsp Grand Marnier or Cointreau

Heat the oven to 160C/325F/Gas 3. Butter a 9½ inch/24cm springform cake tin and line the bottom with a round of baking parchment. Finely grind the 4oz/1 cup/120g of the hazelnuts with the flour in a food processor. Melt the butter and the chocolate either in a microwave or in a bowl over a pan of barely simmering water and stir until smooth.

Whisk the egg yolks and half the sugar until pale and thick. Stir in the melted chocolate mixture, the ground hazelnut mixture and the orange zest.

Put the egg whites in a large and scrupulously clean bowl and whisk until soft peaks form — that is, when you lift up some of the egg white with the whisk it forms a soft, slightly drooping peak. Start whisking in the rest of the sugar, 1 tbsp at a time, and whisking well after each addition until stiff and glossy. Gently fold this meringue into the chocolate mixture in two batches, until the two mixtures are evenly combined. Pour the cake mixture into the buttered cake tin and bake for about 45 minutes, until a toothpick or skewer pushed into the middle of the cake comes out dry. Let the cake cool completely before unmoulding.

While the cake is cooling, make the glaze. Heat the cream until just below boiling point, then turn off the heat and stir in the chocolate until melted and smooth. Stir in the syrup and alcohol and leave to cool for about half an hour until thickened.

When the cake has cooled, spread the glaze evenly over the top and the sides of the cake and decorate with the rest of the roasted hazelnuts.

NOTE To roast and skin hazelnuts: spread the nuts in a single layer on a baking tray and bake at 180C/350F/Gas 4 for about 10 minutes. Cool slightly before wrapping the warm nuts in a tea towel and rubbing them vigorously in the cloth to loosen as much of the skins as possible.

The cake can be made a day in advance, but keep it at room temperature — the fridge will kill it.

EIGHT SERVINGS

GERMAN PLUM CAKE

The burnished plum topping, glistening with its spiced glaze, makes this a most tempting looking cake. Don't be alarmed at its rather unconventional construction; we were, but can now assure you that this is a recipe which works and is a huge hit with all who taste it. We owe its discovery to Stephanie Alexander in her *The Cook's Companion*.

for the cake
3oz/¾ sticks/90g butter, softened
3oz/½ cup/90g caster/granulated sugar
4½oz/1⅛ cups/135g plain/all-purpose flour
1 tsp baking powder
pinch of salt
2 free-range eggs, beaten
1fl oz/2 tbsp/30 ml milk
1½oz/⅜ cup/45g ground almonds
10 plums, halved and stoned

for the topping
1½oz/3 tbsp/45g butter
2½oz/½ cup/75g caster/granulated sugar
1½ tsp ground cinnamon
2 free-range eggs, beaten

Heat the oven to 180C/375F/Gas 4. Butter a 9½ inch/24cm springform cake tin and line the bottom with a round of baking parchment. Beat the softened butter with the sugar until light and creamy. Sift the flour, baking powder and salt together. Whisk the eggs and the milk together. Beat the flour and the egg-milk mixture into the creamed butter in alternate spoonfuls until well-mixed. Spoon the cake mixture into the buttered cake tin and sprinkle evenly with the ground almonds. Arrange the plums, cut side up, on top.

To make the topping, melt the butter, stir in the sugar and spice and cool slightly before beating in the eggs. Spoon the topping over and around the plums on the cake, put into the oven and bake for about an hour, or until a toothpick or skewer inserted into the middle of the cake comes out dry. Cool slightly before unmoulding. Best eaten warm, with fromage frais (for the restrained) or vanilla ice-cream (for the indulgent).

NOTE The cake reheats very well, either in the microwave or wrapped in foil in a 180C/350F/Gas 4 oven for 15 minutes.

EIGHT SERVINGS

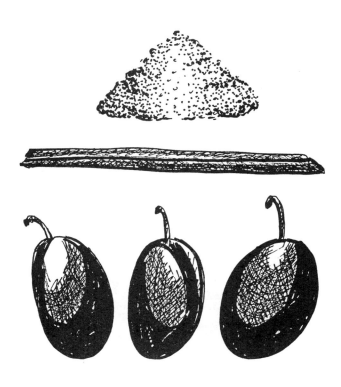

APRICOT CUSTARD TART

A lovely tart from Emily Luchetti's *Four Star Desserts*. If you can't find ripe apricots, use tinned. Or you could substitute ripe peach or mango slices. The important thing is that the fruit is ripe. Patricia Wells in *At Home in Provence* also makes an apricot custard tart, but uses 2 tbsp of lavender honey instead of the sugar, which you might like to try too.

10 ripe apricots
6oz/1 cup/180g caster/granulated sugar
2 free-range egg yolks
2 tbsp plain/all-purpose flour
6fl oz/¾ cup/180ml double/heavy cream
½ tsp natural vanilla extract
1oz/¼ cup/30g flaked/sliced almonds
9½ inch/24cm sweet pastry case baked blind/pre-baked
(see pages 122-4)

Heat the oven to 160C/325F/Gas 3. Halve, stone, and quarter the apricots. Arrange them, as prettily as possible, cut side up, in concentric circles, on the pastry case. Whisk the sugar and eggs together, then whisk in the flour, then the cream and vanilla. Pour this custard over the apricots, sprinkle evenly with almonds and bake until the custard has just set, about 40 minutes. Serve warm or cold, sprinkled with icing (confectioners') sugar.

EIGHT SERVINGS

CHERRY ALMOND TART

Other summer fruits which lend themselves to this recipe from Patricia Wells' *At Home in Provence* are ripe apricots and peaches. But using juicy, seedless, thin-skinned grapes, white, red or black, means you can enjoy this subtle, perfumed tart well into the autumn months.

1lb/500g fresh cherries, pitted
1 free-range egg, beaten
2oz/5 tbsp/60g caster/granulated sugar
1 tbsp plain/all-purpose flour
4 tbsp ground almonds
4fl oz/½ cup/120ml double/heavy cream
½ tsp natural almond extract
1 tsp natural vanilla extract
9½ inch/24cm sweet pastry case baked blind/pre-baked
(see pages 122-4)

Put a baking tray in the oven, and heat to 180C/350F/Gas 4. Whisk the egg, sugar, flour and almonds together, then stir in the cream and flavourings. Sprinkle the other 2 tbsp of ground almonds over the base of the pastry case (this is to absorb any fruit juices and thus prevent soggy pastry). Arrange the cherries in a single layer in the pastry case and pour over the almond-cream filling. Put the tart into the oven on to the hot baking tray (yet another ruse to avoid soggy pastry) and bake until the filling has nicely coloured and set, about 45 minutes. Cool before serving, dusted with icing (confectioners') sugar, with a generous spoonful of fromage frais.

NOTE   Best eaten on the day of baking.

EIGHT SERVINGS

STICKY DATE & CHOCOLATE PUDDING
WITH BUTTERSCOTCH SAUCE

A runaway winner from Andrew Blake's *Blakes*. Sticky toffee puddings are good — this we all agree — but sticky toffee puddings with chocolate are better.

for the sauce
6oz/1½ cups/180g soft brown sugar
4oz/1 stick/120g butter
4fl oz/½ cup/120ml double/heavy cream

for the pudding
6oz/180g pitted dates
1½ tsp bicarbonate of soda/baking soda
14fl oz/1¾ cups/420ml boiling water
3oz/¾ stick/90g butter, softened
4oz/120g soft brown sugar
1½ tsp natural vanilla extract
2 free-range eggs, beaten
10oz/2¼ cups/300g plain/all-purpose flour
2 tsp baking powder
8oz/240g plain/bittersweet chocolate, roughly chopped

Heat the oven to 180C/350F/Gas 4. Butter and line a 9½ inch/ 24cm cake tin — either a *moule à manquer* or a springform tin. Heat the butterscotch ingredients together until the sugar has completely dissolved and the sauce is bubbling. Pour half of the sauce into the cake tin and keep the rest to serve with the pudding.

Put the dates and bicarbonate of soda into a bowl and pour over the boiling water. Beat the butter until it is pale and soft, then add the sugar and vanilla and beat until light and creamy. Beat in the eggs, a little at a time, then stir in the dates and their water. Sift the flour and baking powder into this mixture and gradually fold together to make a smooth batter. Stir in the chocolate and pour together to make a smooth batter. Pour the mixture into the cake tin and bake for 30 minutes before turning down the oven to 160C/325F/Gas 3 and cooking for about an hour. When cooked, a skewer or toothpick pushed into the middle of the pudding should come out dry.

Heat the rest of the sauce until nicely bubbling; spoon this lovely sticky sauce over thick wedges of the hot pudding and complete ultimate indulgence with a big blob of crème fraîche. Yum.

NOTE   A cake which reheats well. Pour some of the sauce over a slice and give a quick blast in the microwave.

EIGHT SERVINGS

MOLASSES CHEESECAKE

A lightly spiced cheesecake which cooks to a deep gold colour and a wickedly velvet texture from Annie Bell's *More Taste Than Time*.

for the crust
6oz/180g gingersnaps, crushed
2oz/4 tbsp/60g butter, melted

for the filling
1¼lb/600g cream cheese, softened
6oz/¾ cup/180g sugar
3 free-range eggs, beaten
¼ pint/⅔ cup/150ml sour cream
½ tsp natural vanilla extract
pinch of salt
½ tsp ground ginger
½ tsp cinnamon
1 tbsp molasses or black treacle

Heat the oven to 160C/325F/Gas 3. Put a dish of hot water on the bottom rack of the oven — this will stop a skin forming on the cheesecake. Mix together the biscuit crumbs and the butter and press evenly into the bottom of a 9½ inch/24cm springform cake tin.

Make the filling using either the paddle attachment on a food mixer, the pulse button on a food processor or a rubber spatula in your hand. Begin by beating the cream cheese until smooth — if you are doing this by hand it is easier if the cream cheese is at room temperature. Then beat in the sugar, then the eggs, then the cream with all the flavourings.

Pour the filling into the cake tin and cook until all but the very centre of the cheesecake is set (don't worry about the wobbly bit in the middle as it will carry on cooking as it cools), 30-40 minutes. Run a knife around the edge of the tin to free the filling from the sides; do this straightaway because, as the cheesecake cools and sets, it also shrinks and, if it is stuck to the sides of the tin, it will split in the middle, which is not pretty. Cool completely before chilling for at least 3 hours or, better still, overnight.

NOTE   The cheesecake will keep very well for a couple of days in the fridge.

EIGHT SERVINGS

URSULA'S CHOCOLATE FANTASY CAKE

One journalist, noting how new recipes are tested and new ideas tried out on willing customers and shop staff, compared the Books for Cooks kitchen to a culinary laboratory. How right he was. This cake is the fruit of long and focused (on the part of Ursula) and extremely pleasurable (on the part of customers and staff) experimentation, as, over a period of months, a number of chocolate fantasy prototypes emerged fresh and fragrant from the oven to be tasted and assessed. (Yes, we know, it's a tough job but someone's gotta do it.) And then one day, after such long and arduous culinary exertions, it happens, gastronomic alchemy: the key to chocolate heaven.

16oz/500g plain/bittersweet chocolate
4oz/1 stick/120g butter
6 free-range eggs, separated
3oz/90g caster/granulated sugar
5fl oz/⅔ cup/150ml double/heavy cream
2 tbsp rum
1 tsp natural vanilla extract

Heat the oven to 180C/350F/Gas 4. Butter and flour a 9½ inch/ 24cm springform cake tin. Melt the butter and the chocolate either in a microwave or in a bowl over a pan of barely simmering water and stir until smooth. Whisk the egg yolks and the sugar until pale and thick. Stir in the cream, cooled melted chocolate mixture, rum and vanilla.

Put the egg whites in a large and scrupulously clean bowl and whisk until soft peaks form — that is, when you lift up some of the egg white with the whisk it forms a soft, slightly drooping peak. Gently fold the beaten whites into the chocolate mixture in three batches, until the two mixtures are evenly combined. Pour the cake mixture into the buttered cake tin and bake for 25 minutes, when it should be just set. Let the cake cool completely (at least an hour) before unmoulding. Nicest of all served with thick cream and ripe raspberries.

NOTE   This cake keeps very well — in fact for up to a week — and Ursula maintains that its flavour even matures and improves with keeping.

EIGHT SERVINGS

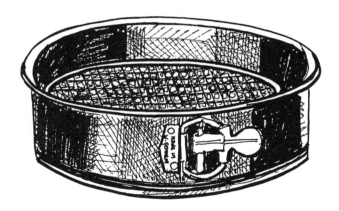

BANANA CARDAMOM CAKE

This is a first class banana cake, and a great favourite of Celia's — she likes to bake it in a bundt pan. Ideal morning coffee or tea time fare with a spoonful of thick, creamy yoghurt, it makes gorgeous pudding on the banana split theme: serve with a scoop of vanilla ice cream and a swirl each of melted dark and white chocolate. From Emily Luchetti's *Four Star Desserts*.

2 very ripe bananas, peeled
4 free-range eggs, separated
2 tsp natural vanilla extract
3fl oz/6 tbsp/90ml sour cream
12oz/3 cups/360g plain/all-purpose flour
2 tsp baking powder
½ tsp salt
2 tsp ground cardamom
6oz/1½ sticks/180g butter, softened
6oz/1 cup/180g dark brown sugar
6 tbsp caster/granulated sugar

Heat the oven to 160C/325F/Gas 3. Butter a 9½ inch/24cm springform cake tin and line the bottom with a round of baking parchment. Mash the bananas and mix in the egg yolks, vanilla and sour cream. Sift the flour with the baking powder, salt and spice.

Beat the softened butter with the brown sugar until light and creamy. Add about half the banana mixture and half the flour mixture to the creamed butter and (either by hand or on the lowest speed of a mixer) work them all together until almost combined. Then add the rest of the banana and flour mixtures, again being careful not to overmix.

Put the egg whites in a large and scrupulously clean bowl and whisk until soft peaks form — that is, when you lift up some of the egg white with the whisk it forms a soft, slightly drooping peak. Start whisking in the rest of the sugar, 1 tbsp at a time, and whisking well after each addition until stiff and glossy. Gently fold this meringue into the banana mixture in two batches. Spoon the cake mixture into the buttered cake tin and bake for about an hour, until a toothpick or skewer pushed into the middle of the cake comes out dry. Let the cake cool completely before unmoulding.

NOTE The cake can certainly be made the day before; when completely cooled, wrap it in cling film but don't put it in the fridge because chilling is quite simply death to cakes.

JENNIFER'S PASTRY-WRAPPED CHIANTI-POACHED PEARS

Jennifer points out that if you leave the pears to cool completely in their syrup overnight, their red wine colour is even deeper and more dramatic. You can of course finish at that stage and not bother with wrapping them in pastry, but serve them well chilled in a glass dish with the syrup spooned over. Both *poires Belle-Angevine* and *douillons* (fruit dumplings from Normandy) are classics of French cooking, but Jennifer stamps them with her own personal touch by choosing Italian wine and enclosing the pears not in a single piece of pastry but in winding strips which shrink and open, making a pretty pattern and giving glimpses of the red pears beneath.

8 firm, tall and slender pears, such as Conference
6oz/1 cup/180g caster/granulated sugar
1¾ pints/4 cups/1 litre Chianti or other Italian red wine
juice and thinly pared peel of 1 orange
1 cinnamon stick
½ tsp black peppercorns
2 cloves
1 vanilla bean, cut in half lengthwise
lemon juice and more sugar if necessary
1lb/500g puff pastry
1 free-range egg beaten
caster/granulated sugar and ground cinnamon for sprinkling

Choose a saucepan in which the pears fit nice and snugly on their sides and cut a round of greaseproof paper which fits the pan exactly. Put the sugar and wine in the pan and warm, stirring until the sugar has completely dissolved. Add all the flavourings, bring to the boil and simmer steadily for 10 minutes, then turn down the heat so that the syrup barely bubbles. Peel the pears and scoop out the flower end with a teaspoon, but leave the stalk on. Cut a thin slice from the bottom of each pear so that they can stand upright. Put the pears in the red wine syrup (adding boiling water if needs be so that they are completely covered) and press the round of paper on top to keep them fully immersed. Put the lid on the pan and poach very gently for 20-45 minutes or until just tender. The exact cooking time depends both on the variety and the ripeness of the pears, but 20 minutes is the minimum to prevent discolouration around the cores. Let the pears cool to tepid in the syrup, then drain and chill them.

Strain the syrup and reduce over a high heat until glossy and thick enough to coat the back of a spoon, about 10 minutes. Correct the seasoning with sugar and lemon juice. Cool.

Heat the oven to 200C/400F/Gas 6. On a lightly floured surface, roll out the pastry to a 10 by 14 inch/25 by 35 cm rectangle and cut lengthwise into ½ inch/1½ cm strips (use a fluted pastry wheel if you have one). Chill the pastry strips for 15 minutes. Now wrap the chilled pears. Put the end of a pastry strip underneath one of the pears and start wrapping it around the pear like a mummy. When it runs out, stick on another pastry strip with beaten egg and carry on wrapping up the pear, finishing at the stalk. When you've wrapped all the pears, brush the pastry all over with beaten egg and put them into the oven to bake until golden brown, about half an hour. Take them out of the oven and straightaway sprinkle them with sugar and cinnamon (a small sieve is best for this). Cool before serving with a spoonful of mascarpone and the red wine syrup spooned over and around.

EIGHT SERVINGS

CRANBERRY CRUMBLE TART

A lovely homely tart, with a fresh, fruity flavour and bright colour, as the filling bubbles up and the deep red juices stain the golden crumble. One word of caution though, some sweet-toothed males in our tasting gatherings found this too tart a tart, although they were outvoted by the majority. So, if you recognise this particular palate among your nearest and dearest, we suggest an apple crumble tart: use six peeled, quartered, cored and sliced eating apples with no sugar and lemon zest instead of orange. From Anna Thomas' *From Anna's Kitchen.*

for the filling
1lb/500g cranberries
4oz/¾ cup/120g sugar
grated zest of 1 orange
a pinch of cinnamon
a pinch of salt

for the crumble
3oz/6 tbsp/90g butter
3oz/¾ cup/90g flour
3oz/¾ cup/90g ground almonds
6oz/1 cup/180g granulated sugar

9½ inch/24cm sweet pastry case baked blind/pre-baked
(see pages 122-4)

Heat the oven to 190C/375F/Gas 5. Pick the cranberries over and chuck out any soft or shrivelled ones. Mix them with the rest of the filling ingredients until they are evenly coated with sugar and spice. Put them into the pastry case, heaping them up a little in the middle. Make the crumble by working the butter into the flour and almonds until it looks nice and crumbly — do this with your fingertips or in a food processor. Stir in the sugar. Distribute evenly over the cranberries. Don't be unduly concerned if the filling looks heaped very high, it will sink as it cooks. Bake the tart until the crumble is a nice golden brown by which time the cranberries will have cooked, about 40 minutes. Cool completely before serving with thick cream.

EIGHT SERVINGS

CELIA'S CHOCOLATE BANANA
MASCARPONE CHEESECAKE

Celia confected this sensational dessert in homage to one of her favourite flavour combinations — and one tiny taste of this cheesecake leaves no doubt that banana and chocolate are a food match made in heaven.

for the crust
7oz/200g plain/dark chocolate digestive/whole wheat
biscuits, crushed
2oz/4 tbsp/60g butter, melted

for the filling
1lb/500g cream cheese, softened
8oz/240g caster/granulated sugar
2 free-range eggs, beaten
8 oz/1 cup/250g mascarpone
2 tsp natural vanilla extract
2 ripe but not brown bananas, sliced

for the topping
3oz/90g plain/bittersweet chocolate
2oz/4 tbsp/60g butter
1 banana
juice of ½ lemon

Heat the oven to 180C/350F/Gas 4. Mix together the biscuit crumbs and the butter and press evenly into the bottom of a 9½ inch/24cm springform cake tin. Bake the crust for 10 minutes and let it cool while you make the filling.

Turn down the oven to 160C/325F/Gas 3. Put a dish of hot water on the bottom rack of the oven — this will stop a skin forming on the cheesecake. Make the filling using either the paddle attachment on a food mixer, the pulse button on a food processor or a rubber spatula in your hand. Begin by beating the cream cheese until smooth — if you are doing this by hand it is easier if the cream cheese is at room temperature. Then beat in the sugar, then the eggs, then the mascarpone with the vanilla and bananas.

Pour the filling into the cake tin and cook until all but the very centre of the cheesecake is set (don't worry about the wobbly bit in the middle as it will carry on cooking as it cools), about 30-40 minutes. Run a knife around the edge of the tin to free the filling from the sides; do this straightaway because, as the cheesecake cools and sets, it also shrinks and, if it is stuck to the sides of the tin, it will split in the middle, which is not pretty. Cool completely before chilling for at least 3 hours or, better still, overnight.

About an hour before you want to serve the cheesecake, melt the chocolate and the butter together either in a microwave or in a bowl over a pan of barely simmering water and stir until smooth. Slice the banana slices attractively on a slight diagonal and immerse them in the lemon juice to discourage discolouration. Carefully unmould the cheesecake and place on a large serving dish. Gently spread the chocolate mixture over the top of the cheesecake — it doesn't matter if it oozes down the sides, in fact we think it looks rather luscious like that. Dry the banana slices on kitchen paper before arranging them on top of the chocolate and chill for another 30 minutes before serving.

NOTE The cheesecake itself can certainly be prepared the day before, but for maximum effect it is better to top it with chocolate and banana not too long in advance.

EIGHT SERVINGS

VICTORIA'S SWEET GOAT'S CHEESE TART

Victoria has been cooking at Books for Cooks since 1992. She maintains that "a Books for Cooks cook must be ready for anything — trying out recipes from books, of course, but also creating dishes from customer's ideas or the unusual ingredients which often find their way into the kitchen. I owe this recipe to Curzon Tussaud, a great cook, friend and faithful Books for Cooks customer."

8oz/250g fresh mild goat's cheese (in a tub rather than a log)
8oz/250g cream cheese
4oz/¾ cup/120g caster/granulated sugar
grated zest of ½ orange
½ tsp vanilla extract
2 free-range eggs, separated
2 tbsp double/heavy cream
1oz/¼ cup/30g flaked/sliced almonds
9½ inch/24cm sweet pastry case baked blind/pre-baked
(see pages 122-4)

Put a baking tray into the oven and heat to 180C/350F/Gas 4. Beat the cheeses with the sugar, orange zest and vanilla until absolutely smooth and lump-free. Work in the egg yolks one by one, then stir in the cream until well mixed. Whisk the egg whites until stiff and lightly but thoroughly fold into the cream-cheese mixture. Pour into the tart case and sprinkle evenly with flaked almonds. Put the tart into the oven on the hot baking tray and straightaway turn the oven down to 160C/325F/Gas 3. Bake until just set, about 20 minutes. Don't worry if the tart still wobbles a little in the middle as it will set as it cools. Dust with icing sugar and serve warm or cold, but certainly not chilled. Victoria likes to serve this goat's cheese tart with a scoop of fresh berry sorbet for a lovely summer dessert, or with caramel sautéed plums to complete a spendid winter pudding.

EIGHT SERVINGS

ORANGE & ALMOND CAKE

The absolute apotheosis of orange cakes from Claudia Roden's *The Book of Jewish Food*. The cooked whole oranges contribute a citrus fragrance and flavour devoid of any customary citrus sharpness and a stunning colour which makes it look as though you've used the yellowest of eggs. Promote it to dessert status by accompanying each slice with a pile of citrus segments, or serve each slice in a pool of citrus syrup (use the juice and julienned zest of 3 oranges and 1 lemon, 4oz/¾ cup/120g sugar and 4fl oz/¾ cup/120ml water, simmered all together for about 20 minutes).

2 large oranges
6 free-range eggs, beaten
8oz/1⅓ cups/240g caster/granulated sugar
2 tbsp orange flower water
8oz/2 cups/240g ground almonds
1 tsp baking powder

Wash and scrub the oranges before boiling them whole in water to cover for about 1½ hours (half an hour in a pressure cooker) or until completely soft. Cool before cutting them in half and removing any pips. Put them in a food processor and work to a purée.

Heat the oven to 190C/375F/Gas 5. Butter a 9½ inch/24cm springform cake tin and line the bottom with a round of baking parchment. Beat the eggs with the sugar until mixed, then fold in the orange flower water, baking powder, ground almonds and orange purée until evenly combined. Pour the cake mixture into the buttered tin and bake for about 1 hour, or until firm to the touch. Do cook it a little longer if the cake is still very wet. Cool completely before dusting with icing (confectioners') sugar and serving with thick creamy yoghurt.

EIGHT SERVINGS

VICTORIA'S PERFECT PAVLOVA & OTHER FAMOUS BOOKS FOR COOKS MERINGUES STRIKE BACK

Our meringue mission continues with customary vigour and we have reaped a rich harvest from this year's cooking. But first let's get serious with a little technical talk.

A FEW DEFINITIONS

A meringue is defined as a very light confection of whipped egg white and sugar. However, where as a traditional meringue is baked at a low temperature for a long time so that it dries out to a crisp crunchiness all through, Victoria prefers to make "soft" meringues and pavlovas, which differ from the more familiar meringue in having a crisp exterior but a soft interior. What is the difference between a meringue and a pavlova, we hear you cry. Well, to be called a pavlova, the meringue must have the addition of vinegar and cornflour which further softens the interior of the meringue to a sublime marshmallow-ness.

MERINGUE TROUBLE-SHOOTING

There is no question about it, meringues are tricky. A surprisingly high proportion of the culinary crisis calls we receive at Books for Cooks are meringue-related, and it was this fact which prompted us to have a section devoted to meringues in our first little book. And so this year we thought we'd make a little space for Victoria to share with you some tips which have helped her along the way.

There is one contingent factor in meringue-making it is difficult to control, namely the oven. Victoria notices this especially because, as a cookery teacher and caterer, she has to use lots of different ovens. The important thing is to understand the basic principle of pavlova (and soft meringue)-cooking. What you want is a short blast of high heat to set and crisp the outside and then a long period of low heat to set but not certainly not dry out the inside.

If the meringue is too runny to hold its shape or spreads and collapses during cooking, this usually means that either egg whites were not at stiff peaks (that is, when the whites stand up in stiff pointed peaks) when you began to add the sugar or once the sugar had been added the egg whites were not whisked until stiff and glossy enough — remember you should be able to hold the bowl above you head without ending up with a new hair-do.

If sugar weeps in little syrupy droplets as the meringue cooks, forming bubbly outbreaks, this means that sugar wasn't added gradually enough and beaten in thoroughly enough, or that your oven is too hot. If sugar syrup weeps from the meringue once it is cooked, that means it wasn't cooked long enough.

Having enumerated some of the things which do go wrong, let's mention some good and indeed great things about meringues. One such is how convenient they are: you don't need a recipe because the proportions are so easy to remember 1 egg white (1fl oz/2 tbsp/30ml) to double the amount of sugar (2oz/⅓ cup/60g). Leftover egg whites are a real by-product of cooking and, being practically fat-free, they keep for a couple of weeks in a covered bowl in the fridge and indefinitely in the freezer. Even more convenient is that, contrary to the usual rule of freshest is best, old egg whites make better meringues. One thing though, for maximum mile-high volume, they are better whisked at room temperature rather than straight from the fridge. To bring egg whites to room temperature, put them in a bowl over another bowl of warm water, stirring every so often.

Lastly, in a world where we are ever conscious of "a moment on the lips, a lifetime on the hips", meringues are surprisingly low-fat and, garnished with yoghurt or fromage frais and fresh fruit, they remain so. OK, so sugar rots your teeth, but hey, nothing's perfect.

Let's proceed with one classic and several new fangled meringues.

CLASSIC PASSION FRUIT PAVLOVA

An Australian institution, this passion fruit smothered pavlova comes from Stephanie Alexander's *The Cook's Companion*.

6 free-range egg whites, at room temperature
a pinch of salt
12oz/2 cups/360g caster/superfine sugar
2 tsp cornflour
1 tsp vinegar
8fl oz/1 cup/240ml double/heavy cream
15 passion fruit

Heat the oven to 180C/350F/Gas 4. Lightly grease a baking tray and line it with baking parchment. Draw an 8½ inch (22cm) circle on the paper.

Put the egg whites in a large, clean, grease-free bowl with a pinch of salt and whisk until stiff. Start whisking in the sugar, 1 tbsp at a time, and whisking well after each addition. Continue whisking until the egg whites are stiff and glossy — this is all important, they should be stiff enough for you to hold the bowl over your head without the meringue falling out. Last of all, whisk in the cornflour and vinegar. Mound the meringue on to the paper lined tray within the circle and smooth the top and sides. Bake the meringue for 5 minutes and then turn the oven down to 130C/250F/Gas 1 and cook for an hour and a quarter until crunchy-crusted but still marshmallow-centred. Cool completely before carefully lifting off the baking parchment. A real aussie or kiwi would now turn the pavlova upside-down to garnish it, but it is so much prettier right side up, and in this case aesthetics wins over authenticity. Cut the passion fruit in half crosswise (easiest with a serrated knife) and scoop out the pulp with a teaspoon. Whip the cream until it holds its shape. Spread each pavlova with the whipped cream and spoon over the passion fruit pulp.

EIGHT SERVINGS

LEMON MERINGUE ROULADE

A brilliant variation on a classic dessert and a truly superlative meringue from Jennifer Paterson and Clarissa Dickson Wright's *Two Fat Ladies*. As Victoria points out, you can certainly buy in the shops — and definitely make at home — lots of different sort of fruit curds with which to ring the changes in this first class pudding.

6 free-range egg whites at room temperature
a pinch of salt
12oz/2 cups/360g caster/superfine sugar
1 tsp cornflour
8fl oz/1 cup/240ml double/heavy cream
6 tbsp lemon curd

Heat the oven to 180C/325F/Gas 3. Line a baking tray with greased baking parchment so that the paper stands proud of the edges of the tray by 1 inch/2½cm. Make a stiff meringue with the egg whites, salt and sugar. Fold in the cornflour. Spread the meringue on the lined tray and bake for 20 minutes when the surface of the meringue should be crisp — if it isn't, put it back into the oven until it is. Cool completely before rolling and filling. To turn it out you will need to be a bit brave. Spread another piece of baking parchment rather larger than the tray on your work surface. Lift the meringue out of its tray with the edges of the paper, flip it over and tip out on to the other piece of baking parchment. Carefully peel off the top piece of baking parchment. Whip the cream until it holds its shape. Spread first the cream and then the lemon curd evenly over the meringue. Roll it up like a Swiss roll, starting at the long end and using the paper to help. Finish with a dusting of icing (confectioners') sugar.

EIGHT SERVINGS

CELIA'S RHUBARB & GINGER FOOL MERINGUE

Although born and bred in the USA, Celia is a passionate anglophile. Her special talent is very much in mixing and matching the flavours of her native and adoptive countries. This recipe makes new use of a very traditional English springtime pudding and to great effect: the refreshing slight tartness of the rhubarb fool offsets the sugary meringue to perfection.

6 free-range egg whites at room temperature
a pinch of salt
10oz/1¾ cups/300g caster/superfine sugar
6 pieces of stem ginger, finely chopped
2lb/1kg rhubarb, cut into pieces
grated zest of 1 orange
½ tsp ground ginger
4oz/¾ cup/120g caster/granulated sugar (maybe more)
10fl oz/1¼ cups/300ml double/heavy cream
mint sprigs to decorate

Heat the oven to 180C/350F/Gas 4. Lightly grease and line two baking trays with baking parchment. Draw an 8½ inch/22cm circle on each tray. Use the egg whites, salt and sugar to make a stiff meringue, divide between each circle and bake for 5 minutes before turning the oven down to 130C/250F/Gas 1 and cooking for 1 hour. Cool completely before lifting the meringues off the baking parchment. Put the rhubarb with the sugar, orange zest and ginger in a pan, cover and stew very slowly for 15-20 minutes, stirring every now and then. Then put the cooked rhubarb in a sieve over a bowl to drain off some of the water. Cool completely and correct the sweetness before mashing until smooth-ish. Whip the cream until it holds its shape and then fold in the cooled rhubarb so that the fruit swirls and ripples through the cream rather than mixing them together completely. Sandwich the meringues together with half of the rhubarb fool. Spread the rest of the fool over the top meringue and decorate with mint sprigs, or, if you're a real ginger fan, with slivers of stem ginger.

EIGHT SERVINGS

LITTLE PAVS WITH CLOTTED CREAM,
WILD STRAWBERRIES & ROSE SYRUP

In another of this year's Australian cookbooks, *Blakes,* Andrew Blake re-invents this culinary antipodean classic in a modern Australian style. First make the individual pavlovas from *One Year At Books For Cooks No. 2.* Make a simple sugar syrup by dissolving 3oz/½ cup/90g sugar in 5fl oz/⅔ cup/150ml water, bring it to the boil, add a handful of rose petals and simmer for 10 minutes to infuse. Cool and strain through a sieve before serving. Garnish the baby pavs with the cream and strawberries, spoon over and around the rose syrup and serve with a glass of champagne.

SOPHIE'S CHOCOLATE YOGHURT MERINGUES

Sophie (see *One Year At Book for Cooks No. 2*) is currently working on a book about cooking with yoghurt, so we though we'd let you have a little preview. Actually what is so very good about this recipe is not that the sheer indulgence of these meringues is atoned for by the yoghurt in terms of calories, but that the slight sharpness of the yoghurt cuts through the rich ganache and the sweet meringue, making for a wonderful flavour combination, better, actually, than cream.

6 free-range egg whites, at room temperature
a pinch of salt
12oz/1½ cups/360g caster/superfine sugar
1oz/30g cocoa powder
6oz/180g plain/bittersweet chocolate, chopped
5fl oz/⅔ cup/150ml double/heavy cream
16fl oz/2 cups/500ml thick creamy yoghurt

Heat the oven to 180C/350F/Gas 4. Lightly grease a baking tray and line it with baking parchment. Make a stiff meringue with the egg whites, salt and sugar. Fold in the cornflour, vinegar and cocoa and drop generous spoonfuls of meringue: you need 16 meringues in total. Bake the meringues for 5 minutes and then turn down the oven to 130C/250F/Gas 1 and cook for another 45 minutes. Cool completely before carefully lifting off the paper.

While the meringues are baking, make the chocolate ganache. Heat the cream until just below boiling point, then turn off the heat and stir in the chocolate until melted and smooth. Put into the refrigerator to cool until thickened. To assemble, spread half of the meringues first with chocolate ganache, then with yoghurt, then sandwich together with the rest of the meringues. Serve at once.

EIGHT SERVINGS

Basics

Shortcrust & Sweet Pastry

An easy, good-tempered pastry which will line a 9½ inch/24cm tart tin. We urge removable bases because they do make life easier when it comes to unmoulding your finished savoury or sweet tart. In fact, a great tip is to rest the tart tin on an upturned mixing bowl, and the tart will practically unmould itself as the outer metal rim just slips off. All the tarts in this little book, sweet or savoury, require blind baking/pre-baking the pastry case. You will need a baking tray and some baking beans — dried beans or pasta will do just as well as the purpose-built ceramic ones. There are few things more disappointing than soggy undercooked pastry when you have gone to all the trouble of preparing a superlative tart filling, so judge the cooking time by the colour rather than by the clock and bake your pastry case until a light biscuit brown.

SHORTCRUST PASTRY

6oz/1½ cups/180g plain/all-purpose flour, sifted
a good pinch of salt
3oz/¾ stick/90g very cold butter, cubed
1 free-range egg yolk plus 1 tbsp cold water, or 2-4 tbsp
water

Lightly butter a 9½ inch/24cm tart tin and put it into the refrigerator. Put the flour and salt in a food processor and aerate with a couple of quick on/off pulses. Add the butter and process till the mixture resembles fine breadcrumbs. Add the yolk and water (if necessary) and process until the pastry just draws together. Turn it out on to a lightly floured work surface and knead briefly to form a flat round. If you don't have a food processor, do the whole thing as lightly as possible, using your fingertips to rub the butter into the flour and, when you add the liquid, pinching the whole thing into a dough. Unless it's a very hot day, you should roll the pastry out straightaway without chilling first. Line the chilled tin with the pastry lifted into place on the rolling pin, trim the edges with a generous hand as the pastry might shrink, and put into the refrigerator to rest for at least an hour, or into the freezer for 15 minutes, if you're pushed for time. Do not, under any circumstances, throw the leftover pastry away, but roll it into a ball, wrap in cling film and keep at room temperature until you take your baked pastry case out of the oven (see pastry problems below).

SWEET PASTRY

Use the quantities and method given above, but mix in 1½oz/5 tbsp/45g sifted icing (confectioners') sugar with the flour and salt, and add ½ tsp vanilla essence with the egg yolk and, if necessary, water. We advise using icing (confectioners') sugar as its fine starchiness, as opposed to the graininess of ordinary sugar, contributes to the pastry's manageability.

BAKING BLIND (PRE-BAKING)

Put a baking tray in the oven and heat to 190C/375F/Gas 5. Having a hot baking tray in the oven helps the pastry case cook more evenly, otherwise the sides tend to cook before the base. Line the chilled pastry case with baking parchment, fill with baking beans and cook for 10 minutes. Carefully remove the beans and paper and cook for another 10 minutes or a little longer, until a light biscuit brown.

PASTRY PROBLEMS

Having everything very cold really helps; you might like to put your butter cubes in the freezer for 5 minutes extra chilling to keep everything nice and cold, while some people keep their flour in the freezer both for pastry purposes and because it keeps better.

If your pastry is too crumbly, roll it out between two pieces of cling film/plastic wrap. If it is too soft because the ingredients are too warm, or you have added too much liquid, chill it first, until firm but not rock-hard, before rolling out in between cling film.

Cling film, as you can see, is but a little short of a universal panacea, working wonders with all kinds of pastry problems.

Well, you lined the tin, rested the pastry and baked it blind. Hopefully you now have a perfect pastry case before you. If, however, you find you have a less than perfect pastry case with one or two or lots of little cracks in it (evil little cracks through which the tart filling threatens to seep), do not despair. This is where your leftover pastry will come to the rescue. Gently press scraps of the leftover raw pastry to the cracks in the hot pastry shell and the heat will stick the raw and the cooked pastry together and seal up the cracks. Easy as pie.

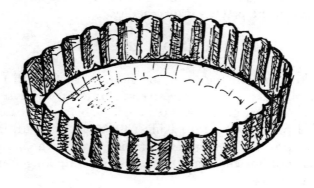

MENUS

CELIA'S MENU

Creamy Madeira Mushrooms with Apple

Grilled Aubergine & Polenta Stacks with Beetroot Salsa

Chocolate Banana Mascarpone Cheesecake

JENNIFER'S MENU

Warm Roasted Tomato Bruschetta with Red Onion & Basil Vinaigrette

*Chicken Thighs Stewed in Balsamic Vinegar with Porcini
Mushrooms & Sun-Dried Cherries served with Roasted
Garlic Potato Purée*

Pastry-Wrapped Chianti-Poached Pears

URSULA'S MENU

Polpette di Melanzane

Spinach, Fennel & Tomato Lasagne

Chocolate Fantasy Cake

VICTORIA'S MENU

*Salad of Smoked Fish, Roasted Cherry Tomatoes & Rocket
with Chervil-Dill Vinaigrette*

Marinated Fillet of Lamb with Coriander-Yoghurt Sauce

Sweet Goat's Cheese Tart

OUR FAVOURITE FOOD SHOPS

These are the shops local to Books for Cooks which we really couldn't do without. If you are coming to visit us, we strongly advise a visit to at least one of them as well.

Archie Foodstore
14 Moscow Rd, W2
0171-229-2275
Mon-Sun 8am-8pm
An real Aladdin's cave of Middle Eastern ingredients, fruit and vegetables as well as groceries — *and* pomegranate syrup!

Garcia R. & Sons
248 Portobello Road, W11
0171-221-6119
Mon-Wed, Fri, Sat 9am-6pm;
Thur 9am-1.30pm
A Spanish delicatessan which is a Portobello institution — our favourite shop of them all.

Michanicou Brothers
2 Clarendon Rd, W11
0171-727-5191
Mon-Fri 9am-6.30pm
Sat 9am-5.30pm
Excellent specialist greengrocer: wild rocket vine-ripened tomatoes, you name it.

Planet Organic
42 Westbourne Grove, W2
0171-221-7171
Mon-Sat 9am-8pm
Sun 1pm-5pm
At last, a fully organic supermarket

Portobello Fruit & Vegetable Market
Portobello Road, W11
Mon-Wed 9am-5pm
Thur 9am-1pm
The test kitchen could never have even come into existence without the market. Friday is the best day, and Brian keeps the stall to go for, in between Blenheim and Elgin Crescents.

The Spice Shop
1 Blenheim Crescent, W11
0171-221-4448
Mon-Sat 9.30am-6pm
Mind-boggling, nose-twitching array of spices, right opposite Books for Cooks, and they send too.

Tawana
16-20 Chepstow Rd, W2
0171-221-6316
Mon-Sun 9.30am-8pm
Tremendous selection of Thai ingredients, including fresh fruit and vegetables.

Wild Oats
210 Westbourne Grove, W11
0171-229-1063
Mon-Wed, Fri 9am-7pm
Tues 10am-7pm Sat 9am-6pm
Sun 10am-5pm
Much more than just a healthfood shop.

FOOD IN SEASON

This listing is our attempt to indicate when British ingredients are at their very best. We are increasingly concerned by the current blurring of the seasons, and feedback from customers suggests that we are not alone in this concern. All year availability for everything may be frightfully convenient, but, in addition to question marks over quality and cost, much of the joy of cooking and eating is dampened by the lack of anything to look forward to. Simple pleasures like ripe, red summer strawberries and cream, the sweet crunch of an autumn apple, springtime tender asparagus or fresh crab with egg-rich mayonnaise, a warming winter mash of floury potatoes, salt butter and hot milk, and most sadly and wastefully of all, wild salmon, are blunted by over-familiarity with these seasonal foodstuffs, while certain culinary traditions risk being lost when there is no arrival and no noticeable abundance of ingredients to celebrate. Hopefully, this information will enable you and us to shop, cook and eat in greater harmony with the British food calendar.

The list is far from definitive, especially for fish, where we've focused on what we use most. However, monkfish, which we cook a lot, appears to be without notable seasons and is therefore not listed. Cauliflowers too, are in season year round as there are different varieties cultivated for different times of year. Nor have we mentioned beef, pork, chicken or even duck because they are very constantly available without any noticeable variation in quality. Lamb is a different matter and we've noted the key points in the year when it's really good eating and should definitely be sought out. Don't fall for force-reared, so-called new season lamb at Easter; it's never seen grass and has only eaten pellets, so wait until the end of May. Weaned lamb (hogget) is at its best in September-October, when it's sweet and succulent, or in February-March, when it's developed a really full flavour.

We are in no way suggesting that imported ingredients should be shunned, just that full advantage is taken of home-grown foodstuffs when they are at their best. Imported fruit and vegetables have always played an important role in the British culinary calendar: imagine, no bitter oranges from Seville, no marmalade at breakfast. Indeed it is sometimes not only preferable to choose an imported product over a home-grown one (think aubergines, peppers) but actually imperative: in the early months of the year imported fruit really saves the day due to the scarceness of anything home-grown. In fact, when you look at that part of the food calendar (known by gardeners as "the hungry gap"), you understand why the British became a nation of great preservers!

BRITISH FOOD CALENDAR

JANUARY
FRUIT apples (dessert, cooking) pears, rhubarb (forced)
VEGETABLES artichokes (jerusalem), beetroot, brussel sprouts, cabbages (green, red, savoy, white), cardoons, carrots, celeriac, chard, chicory, curly kale, leeks, mushrooms (browncap), onions (maincrop), parsnips, potatoes (maincrop), salsify, seakale, shallots, spring greens, swede, turnips
FISH cod, dover sole, grey mullet, haddock, halibut, lemon sole, oysters, scallops, turbot
POULTRY goose, guinea-fowl, turkey
GAME hare, pheasant, pigeon, rabbit, snipe, venison

FEBRUARY
FRUIT apples (dessert, cooking), pears, rhubarb (forced)
VEGETABLES artichokes (jerusalem), beetroot, brussel sprouts, cabbages (green, red, savoy, white), cardoons, carrots, celeriac, chard, chicory, curly kale, leeks, mushrooms (browncap), onions (maincrop), parsnips, potatoes (maincrop), salsify, seakale, shallots, spring greens, swede, turnips, watercress
FISH cod, dover sole, grey mullet, haddock, halibut, lemon sole, oysters, scallops, turbot
POULTRY goose
MEAT lamb (hogget)
GAME pigeon, rabbit, venison

MARCH

FRUIT apples (dessert, cooking), pears, rhubarb
VEGETABLES artichokes (jerusalem), beetroot, broccoli (sprouting), cabbages (green), carrots, chicory, cucumbers, leeks, mushrooms (browncap), onions (maincrop), parsnips, potatoes (maincrop), seakale, shallots, spring greens, swede, turnips, watercress
FISH halibut, lemon sole, mussels, oysters, scallops, sea trout, shrimp
MEAT lamb (hogget)

APRIL

FRUIT apples (cooking), rhubarb
VEGETABLES broccoli (sprouting), cabbages (spring green), carrots, cucumbers, leeks, mushrooms (browncap), potatoes (maincrop), radishes, seakale, sorrel, spinach, spring greens, swede, watercress
FISH brown trout, crab, halibut, lemon sole, lobster, mussels, prawns, oysters, salmon, sea trout, shrimp

MAY

FRUIT apples (cooking), gooseberries, rhubarb
VEGETABLES asparagus, broccoli (sprouting), cucumbers, kohlrabi, mushrooms (browncap), potatoes (maincrop), radishes, rocket, sorrel, spinach, spring greens, spring onions, watercress
FISH brown trout, crab, haddock, lobster, mussels, prawns, salmon, sea trout, shrimp
MEAT lamb (new season)

JUNE

FRUIT apples (cooking), cherries, gooseberries, rhubarb, strawberries
VEGETABLES asparagus, beans (broad), broccoli, carrots (new season), celery, courgettes, cucumbers, lettuce, peas, potatoes (new), radishes, rocket, sorrel, spinach, spring onions, turnips (new season)
FISH bass, brown trout, crab, dover sole, grilse (young salmon), haddock, lobster, prawns, salmon, sea trout, shrimp
POULTRY duckling
MEAT lamb (new season)

JULY

FRUIT *bilberries, blackcurrants, blueberries, cherries (morello, sweet), gooseberries, loganberries, raspberries, redcurrants, strawberries, whitecurrants,*

VEGETABLES *artichokes (globe), beans (broad, french, runner), beetroot (new season), broccoli, carrots, celery, chard, courgettes, cucumbers, kohlrabi, lettuce, peas, potatoes (new), radishes, rocket, sorrel, spinach, spring onions, tomatoes, turnips,*

FISH *bass, brown trout, dover sole, grilse (young salmon), haddock, halibut, grey mullet, lobster, prawns, sea trout, salmon, shrimp*

POULTRY *duckling*

AUGUST

FRUIT *apricots, bilberries, blackberries, blackcurrants, blueberries, cherries, gooseberries, loganberries, mulberries, plums, raspberries, redcurrants, strawberries, whitecurrants*

VEGETABLES *artichokes (globe), beans (broad, french, runner), beetroot, broccoli, carrots, celery, chard, courgettes, cucumbers, kohlrabi, leeks, lettuce, marrows, mushrooms (browncap, wild), onions, (pickling) peas, potatoes (new), radishes, rocket, shallots, sorrel, spinach, spring onions, tomatoes, turnips*

FISH *bass, crab, dover sole, grey mullet, haddock, halibut, lobster, prawns, salmon, shrimp, turbot*

POULTRY *guinea-fowl*

GAME *grouse (from the 12th)*

SEPTEMBER

FRUIT *apples (dessert, cooking), blackberries, blueberries, crabapples, damsons, elderberries, figs, greengages, mulberries, plums, strawberries*

VEGETABLES *artichokes, beans (french, runner), beetroot, broccoli, carrots, celery, chard, chicory, courgettes, cucumber, kohlrabi, leeks, lettuce, marrow, mushrooms (browncap, wild), onions (pickling, maincrop), potatoes (maincrop, new), pumpkins, radishes, rocket, shallots, sorrel, spinach, spring onions, swede, sweetcorn, tomatoes, turnips, watercress*

FISH *bass, cod, dover sole, grey mullet, haddock, halibut, lobster, mussels, prawns, oysters, shrimp, turbot*

POULTRY *guinea-fowl*

MEAT *lamb (hogget)*

GAME *grouse, mallard, pigeon, rabbit*

OCTOBER

FRUIT apples (dessert, cooking), blackberries, crabapples, damsons, hazelnuts, medlars, pears, quinces, sloes, walnuts

VEGETABLES beans (french, runner), beetroot, broccoli, cabbages (green, red, savoy), celeriac, chicory, chard, corn salad, kohlrabi, leeks, lettuce, marrows, mushrooms (browncap, wild), onions (pickling, maincrop), parsnips, potatoes (maincrop), pumpkins, radishes, rocket, shallots, spinach, swede, sweetcorn, turnips, watercress

FISH bass, cod, dover sole, grey mullet, haddock, halibut, mussels, prawns, oysters, shrimp, turbot

POULTRY goose, guinea-fowl

MEAT lamb (hogget)

GAME grouse, hare, partridge, pheasant, pigeon, rabbit, teal, venison

NOVEMBER

FRUIT apples (dessert, cooking), chestnuts, filberts, hazelnuts, medlars, pears, quinces, walnuts

VEGETABLES beetroot, broccoli, brussel sprouts, cabbages (green, red, savoy), celeriac, chard, chicory, corn salad, kohlrabi, leeks, mushrooms (browncap, wild), onions (pickling, maincrop), parsnips, potatoes, pumpkins, shallots, spinach, swede, turnips, watercress

FISH bass, cod, dover sole, grey mullet, haddock, halibut, mackerel, mussels, oysters, turbot

POULTRY goose, guinea-fowl, turkey

GAME hare, mallard, partridge, pheasant, pigeon, rabbit, snipe, woodcock, venison

DECEMBER

FRUIT apples (dessert, cooking), chestnuts, pears, quinces, walnuts

VEGETABLES artichokes (jerusalem), beetroot, brussel sprouts, cabbages (green, red, savoy, white), cardoons, celeriac, chard, chicory, corn salad, curly kale, leeks, mushrooms (browncap, wild), onions (maincrop), parsnips, potatoes, salsify, swede, turnips

FISH bass, cod, dover sole, grey mullet, haddock, halibut, lemon sole, mussels, oysters, scallops, turbot

POULTRY goose, guinea-fowl, turkey

GAME hare, mallard, pheasant, pigeon, rabbit, snipe, venison, woodcock

131

RECIPE LIST

SOUPS

Cream of Fennel Soup 8
Butternut Squash & Pear Soup 9
Chilled Avocado Soup with Tomato Salsa 10
Sweet Onion & Rosemary Soup with Stilton Toasts 12
Tuscan Chickpea & Tomato Soup with Pancetta & Sage 13
Corn Soup with Red Pepper Purée 14
Provençal Winter Vegetable Soup with Parsley Pistou 16
Curried Dhal Soup with Coriander Yoghurt 18

MAIN COURSES

Honey-Glazed Duck with Grapefruit & Ginger Salad 20
Chicken Stewed in Saffron & Fennel with Red Pepper Aioli 22
Smoked Salmon & Lentil Salad with Walnut Vinaigrette 24
Wild Mushroom & Mascarpone Tart with Basil 26
Victoria's Marinated Fillet of Lamb with Coriander-Yoghurt
Sauce 28
Garlic & Goat's Cheese Custards with Grilled Tomato
Sauce 30
Pork Fillet in Ginger Beer Sauce 32
Celia's Creamy Madeira Mushrooms with Apple 33
Lamb Braised in Red Wine with Root Vegetables & Rosemary
Gremolada 34
Chicken & Papaya Salad with Pomegranate Dressing 36
Courgette Fritters with Radish Tzatziki 38
Mildly Spiced Caramelised Onion Tartlets of Hazelnut Pastry with
Tomato & Basil Sauce 40
Thai Chicken with Basil 43
Celeriac Gratin with Tomato-Cream Sauce 44
Jennifer's Chicken Thighs Stewed in Balsamic Vinegar with Porcini
Mushrooms & Sun-Dried Cherries served with Roasted Garlic
Potato Purée 46

Calcutta Fish Cakes 48

Chermoula Marinated Chicken with Spicy Tomato-Honey Sauce & Buttered Couscous 50

Ursula's Polpette di Melanzane 54

Chicken with Walnut Aillade 55

Sweet Soy Glazed Salmon with Cherry Tomato-Cucumber Relish & Soba Noodles 56

Jennifer's Warm Roasted Tomato Bruschetta with Red Onion & Basil Vinaigrette 58

Wine-Braised Guinea Fowl with Prunes & Almonds 60

Paillard of Chicken Breast with Preserved Lemon Couscous & Pistachio Butter 62

Onion & Thyme Tart with Lemon & Herb Dressed Broccoli 64

Victoria's Salad of Smoked Fish, Roasted Cherry Tomatoes & Rocket with Chervil-Dill Vinaigrette 66

Middle Eastern Meat Balls with Smoky Aubergine Purée & Minted Yoghurt 68

Puy Lentils with Dill, Salsa Verde, Roasted Peppers & Feta Cheese 70

Duck Breasts with Sweet Tomato-Sesame Chutney 72

Goat's Cheese, Fennel & Olive Tart with Red Pepper Sauce 74

Celia's Grilled Aubergine & Polenta Stacks with Beetroot Salsa 76

Beef Daube with Mustard, Herbs & White Wine 78

Fennel Gratin with Cream & Parmesan 80

Pistachio-Crusted Fish with Saffron Mashed Potatoes & Masala Sauce 82

Salad of Peppery Greens, Pears, Walnuts & Roquefort with Caramelised Fennel & Onion Bruschelta 84

Barbadian Seasoned Chicken with Avocado Salsa & Gingered Sweet Potato Mash 86

Ursula's Spinach, Fennel & Tomato Lasagne 88

CAKES & TARTS

BASICS

MISCELLANEOUS

NOTES

NOTES